ECONOMICS ABBREVIATIONS DICTIONARY

ECONOMICS ABBREVIATIONS DICTIONARY

Published on 31 October 2024
Copyright ⓒ 2024 by Michael S. Suh (서승종)

Published by Min Seung-won (민승원), INDIEPUP (인디펍㈜)
Publication registration number : 2019-8, 28 January 2019
E-mail : cs@indiepub.kr
Telephone : +82-70-8848-8004
Fax : +82-303-3444-7982
Printed in the Republic of Korea

Price : 30,000 KRW
ISBN 979-11-6756620-1 (13320)

No part of this book may be reproduced in any form without permission from the publisher.

ECONOMICS ABBREVIATIONS DICTIONARY

발행일 2024년 10월 31일
지은이 Michael S. Suh (서승종)

발행처 인디펍
발행인 민승원
출판 등록 2019년 01월 28일 제2019-8호
전자우편 cs@indiepub.kr
대표전화 070-8848-8004
팩스 0303-3444-7982

정가 30,000원
ⓒ Michael S. Suh (서승종)
ISBN 979-11-6756620-1 (13320)

이 책은 저작권법에 따라 보호받는 저작물이므로 무단 전재와 복제를 금합니다.

ECONOMICS ABBREVIATIONS DICTIONARY

Prologue

Economics is life itself. It isn't simply for economics majors or finance professionals; it's a field everyone should understand and apply. From the prices of goods we buy, housing costs, savings, and spending patterns, economics is closely tied to our daily lives. A basic understanding of economics allows us to respond proactively to changing social and market situations. I believe economics is vital knowledge for everyone, empowering us to build a better life. That's why, though a construction engineer, I wanted to organize economic terms. Admittedly, I'm neither an economics major nor a practitioner in the field. There are certainly experts far more qualified academically and practically. Anticipating questions about why a non-specialist would publish a dictionary, I respond: I simply wished to organize and record this information. I aspired to be an 'Archivist,' a professional in record and information management.

Communication happens through spoken and written language. When exchanging specialized information, using abbreviations can facilitate more efficient communication. Those with experience and expertise can generally understand common abbreviations. Yet, for those unfamiliar with these abbreviations, they may seem like codes. Effective communication requires a shared understanding of these abbreviations first, enabling smoother and more efficient exchanges.

In this dictionary, each abbreviation is organized to provide only the core concepts for easy understanding. The abbreviations are systematically arranged with brief explanations, leaving the detailed meanings and professional knowledge for the reader to explore. This dictionary may introduce unfamiliar abbreviations, serving as an opportunity for readers to acquire new knowledge.

Part 1 contains abbreviations related to economics and finance, Part 2 includes business administration terms, and Part 3 focuses on international trade abbreviations. My philosophy is that understanding enables us to read, speak, and write effectively. I hope that readers of this dictionary gain even a small insight into economics and finance, allowing them to experience it indirectly.

I'm grateful to have completed my book before the last leaves fall. I want to express my gratitude to my parents, my beloved wife, and my three children, as well as to everyone who has extended their grace to make me who I am today. Writing has brought me joy, and the thought of continuing to write fills me with excitement.

October 2024
Michael S. Suh (서승종)

CONTENTS

Part 1   Economics and Finance   7

Part 2   Business Administration   171

Part 3   International Trade   215

Index   281

Part 1 Economics and Finance

AB (Accommodation Bill)	25
ABL (Asset Backed Loan)	25
ABS (Asset Backed Securities)	25
ADS (Alternative Depreciation System)	26
ALM (Asset Liability Management)	26
AML (Anti-Money Laundering)	27
AR (Annual Report)	27
AS (Adverse Selection)	28
ASF (Available Stable Funding)	28
BA (Banker's Acceptance)	29
BC (Block Chain)	29
BCR (Benefit Cost Ratio)	30
BE (Bandwagon Effect)	30
BE (Base Effect)	30
BEP (Break Even Point)	31
BIS (Bank for International Settlements)	31
BMS (Budgetary Management System)	31
BOP (Balance of Payments)	32

BPS (Book-value per Share)	32
BR (Bank Run)	33
BS (Balance Sheet)	33
BW (Bond with Warrant)	34
CAPEX (Capital Expenditure)	34
CB (Circuit Breaker)	35
CB (Commercial Bank)	35
CB (Commercial Bill)	36
CB (Convertible Bond)	36
CB (Covered Bond)	36
CBO (Collateralized Bond Obligation)	37
CC (Credit Creation)	37
CC (Credit Crunch)	38
CCB (Contingent Convertible Bond)	38
CCF (Credit Conversion Factor)	39
CCP (Central Counter Party)	39
CCSI (Composite Consumer Sentiment Index)	40
CD (Certificate of Deposit)	40

CD (Countervailing Duties)	40
CD (Credit Derivative)	41
CDO (Collateralized Debt Obligation)	41
CEA (Credit Equivalent Amount)	42
CET1 (Common Equity Tier 1)	42
CF (Crowd Funding)	43
CFC (Common Fund for Commodities)	43
CFS (Cash Flow Statement)	44
CI (Composite Indexes of Business Indicators)	44
CIA (Certified Internal Auditor)	45
CL (Credit Leverage)	45
CLN (Credit Linked Notes)	45
CLO (Collateralized Loan Obligation)	46
CM (Capital Market)	46
CMA (Cash Management Account)	47
CMO (Collateralized Mortgage Obligation)	47
CMS (Cash Management Service)	48
CMS (Credit Management System)	48

CO (Call Option) 49

COFIX (Cost of Funds Index) 49

COGS (Cost of Goods Sold) 50

CP (Capital Productivity) 50

CP (Commercial Paper) 51

CP (Contractionary Policy) 51

CPA (Certified Public Accountant) 51

CPI (Consumer Price Index) 52

CPI (Cost-Push Inflation) 52

CR (Capitalization Rate) 53

CRAs (Credit Ratings Agencies) 53

CS (Credit Spread) 54

CSD (Central Securities Depository) 54

CSI (Consumer Survey Index) 55

CSS (Credit Scoring System) 55

CWM (Chain Weighted Method) 55

D&A (Depreciation and Amortization) 56

DCB (Dual Currency Bond) 56

DDM (Dividend Discount Model)	57
DE (Demonstration Effect)	58
DF (Direct Financing)	58
DLT (Distributed Ledger Technology)	59
DPI (Demand-Pull Inflation)	59
DPI (Disposable Personal Income)	60
DPL (Deposit Placement Line)	60
DR (Depositary Receipts)	61
DSCR (Debt Service Coverage Ratio)	61
DSR (Debt Service Ratio)	62
DTI (Debt to Income Ratio)	62
DVP (Delivery versus Payment)	63
EAD (Exposure at Default)	64
EB (Exchangeable Bond)	64
EBITDA (Earnings Before Interest, Tax, Depreciation, and Amortization)	65
ED (External Debt)	66
EEF (Exchange Equalization Fund)	66
EITC (Earned Income Tax Credit)	67

ELD (Equity Linked Deposit)	67
ELF (Equity Linked Fund)	68
ELS (Equity Linked Security)	69
EM (Electronic Money)	69
EMBI (Emerging Market Bond Index)	70
EMV (Expected Monetary Value)	71
EOS (Economy of Scope)	71
EPS (Earnings per Share)	72
ESI (Export Similarity Index)	72
ETF (Exchange Traded Fund)	73
EURIBOR (Euro Interbank Offered Rate)	74
EVA (Economic Value Added)	74
FC (Factor Cost)	75
FC (Forward Contracts)	75
FD (Final Demand)	76
FD (Financial Derivatives)	76
FE (Fountain Effect)	77

FOP (Free of Payment)	78
FRN (Floating Rate Note)	78
FRS (Fractional Reserve System)	79
FT (Futures Transactions)	79
FV (Face Value)	80
FWM (Fixed Weighted Method)	81
FX (Foreign Exchange)	81
GAAP (Generally Accepted Accounting Principles)	82
GDI (Gross Domestic Investment Ratio)	82
GDP (Gross Domestic Product)	83
GDR (Global Depositary Receipts)	83
GDS (General Depreciation System)	84
GFCF (Gross Fixed Capital Formation)	84
GL (General Ledger)	85
GL (Gross Loss)	85
GMA (Geometric Moving Average)	86
GNI (Gross National Income)	86

GP (General Provisions)	86
GP (Gross Profit)	87
GVA (Gross Value Added)	87
GVC (Global Value Chain)	88
HDI (Household Disposable Income)	89
HE (Hidden Economy)	89
HHI (Herfindahl-Hirschman Index)	90
HSS (Hybrid Settlement System)	90
IB (Investment Bank)	91
IC (Intermediate Consumption)	91
ICO (Initial Coin Offering)	91
IF (Indirect Financing)	92
IFRS (International Financing Reporting Standards)	93
ILG (Income-Led Growth)	93
IOT (Input-Output Tables)	94
IRR (Internal Rate of Return)	94
IRS (Interest Rate Swaps)	95

IT (Impossible Trinity, Impossible Trilemma)	96
JB (Junk Bond)	96
KIKO (Knock-In Knock-Out)	97
KYC (Know Your Customer)	97
LBO (Leveraged Buy Out)	98
LCR (Liquidity Coverage Ratio)	98
LDR (Law of Diminishing Returns)	99
LE (Leverage Effect)	99
LGD (Loss Given Default)	100
LT (Liquidity Trap)	101
LTV (Loan to Value Ratio)	101
MACRS (Modified Accelerated Cost Recovery System)	102
MBS (Mortgage Backed Securities)	102
MMF (Money Market Fund)	103
MOS (Margin of Safety)	104
MPB (Monetary Policy Board)	104
MTM (Mark to Market)	105

MVA (Market Value Added)	106
NCD (Negotiable Certificate of Deposit)	106
NDC (Net Debit Caps)	107
NDF (Non-Deliverable Forward)	107
NDI (National Disposable Income)	108
NEER (Nominal Effective Exchange Rate)	108
NGDP (Nominal Gross Domestic Product)	109
NGT (New Growth Theory)	109
NI (Net Income)	110
NI (Nominal Income)	111
NIM (Net Interest Margin)	112
NL (Net Loss)	112
NM (Natural Monopoly)	113
NNI (Net National Income)	113
NOC (No Occupancy Cost)	114
NOE (Non-Observed Economy)	115
NOI (Net Operating Income)	116

NP (Notional Principal)	117
NPV (Net Present Value)	117
NSFR (Net Stable Funding Ratio)	118
OB (Offshore Banking)	119
OCC (Occupancy)	119
OI (Operating Income)	120
OPEX (Operating Expenditures)	121
ORA (Official Reserve Assets)	122
OS (Operating Surplus)	122
OTC (Over-The-Counter)	123
PAC (Planning Advisory Committee)	123
PB (Protection Buyer)	124
PBR (Price on Book-value Ratio)	125
PD (Probability of Default)	125
PDI (Personal Disposable Income)	126
PED (Price Elasticity of Demand)	126
PER (Price Earnings Ratio)	127

PG (Payment Gateway)	127
PI (Payment Instruments)	128
PI (Property Income)	128
PL (Profit and Loss Statement)	129
PLG (Profit-Led Growth)	129
PM (Primary Market)	130
PO (Put Option)	130
PPI (Producer Price Index)	131
PPP (Purchasing Power Parity)	131
PR (Principal Risk)	132
PS (Protection Seller)	133
PT (Program Trading)	133
PTC (Propensity to Consume)	134
PV (Present Value)	134
PVP (Payment versus Payment)	135
QE (Qualitative Easing)	135
QE (Quantitative Easing)	136

RB (Reserve Base) 136

RCA (Revealed Comparative Advantage) 137

RE (Ratchet Effect) 138

REER (Real Effective Exchange Rate) 138

REITs (Real Estate Investment Trust) 139

RI (Real Income) 139

RML (Reverse Mortgage Loan) 140

ROA (Return on Asset) 140

ROE (Return on Equity) 140

ROI (Return on Investment) 141

ROR (Return on Revenue) 141

RP (Repurchase Agreements) 142

RPS (Retail Payment System) 142

RSF (Required Stable Funding) 143

RT (RegTech; Regulatory Technology) 143

RWA (Risk-Weighted Assets) 144

S&P (Standard & Poor) 144

SAP (System Application and Programs in Data Process)	145
SAS (Statistical Analysis System)	145
SB (Specialized Banking)	146
SB (Straight Bond)	146
SC (Sunk Cost)	147
SC (Supplementary Capital)	147
SCF (Sunk Cost Fallacy)	148
SCM (Supply Chain Management)	149
SDR (Special Drawing Rights)	149
SE (Snob Effect)	150
SEEA (System of Integrated Environmental and Economic Accounts)	150
SF (Settlement Finality)	151
SI (Social Insurance)	151
SIFIs (Systemically Important Financial Institutions)	152
SIO (Stock Index Options)	152
SM (Secondary Market)	153
SNA (System of National Accounts)	153

SO (Smoothing Operation)	154
SO (Stock Option)	155
SOHO (Small Office Home Office)	155
SP (Sterilization Policy)	155
SR (Swap Rate)	156
ST (Security Thread)	156
ST (Stress Test)	157
SU (Statistical Underground)	157
SUT (Supply and Use Tables)	158
SWIFT (Society of Worldwide Interbank Financial Telecommunication)	159
TB (Trading Book)	159
TDE (Trickle-Down Effect)	160
TFR (Total Fertility Rate)	160
TiVA (Trade in Value Added)	161
TRS (Total Return Swap)	162
TSR (Total Share Return)	162
TUE (Trickle-Up Effect)	163

UB (Universal Banking)	163
UE (Underground Economy)	164
USDI (US Dollar Index)	165
VAIC (Value Added Inducement Coefficients)	165
VAR (Value at Risk)	166
VC (Virtual Currency)	166
VE (Veblen's Effect)	167
WACC (Weighted Average Cost of Capital)	167
WLG (Wage-Led Growth)	168
YTM (Yield to Maturity)	168

AB (Accommodation Bill)

AB is a bill issued to enhance creditworthiness, allowing the issuer to secure funds by leveraging another party's credit without an actual transaction. Typically, companies with low credit ratings or difficulty in securing funds use the credit of financial institutions or third parties to obtain capital. ABs rely on the trust between the bill issuer and the third party and are issued solely based on credit without collateral, making them high-risk instruments. Consequently, financial institutions often thoroughly assess the issuer's creditworthiness and repayment capability before the bill's maturity. Accommodation bills are commonly used in credit-oriented financial markets as a means of short-term financing.

ABL (Asset Backed Loan)

ABL refers to a financing method where a company secures loans by using its assets, such as inventory, accounts receivable, or equipment, as collateral. Since the loan is collateralized by assets, lenders evaluate the value and liquidity of these assets to determine the loanable amount. This method enables companies to obtain funds based on asset value, making it particularly useful for businesses with irregular cash flow or significant funding needs, even if their credit rating is low. ABL is advantageous for quickly securing funds in times of liquidity constraints and supports the acquisition of working capital. Loan terms vary according to the collateralized assets, and financial institutions regularly assess asset conditions to manage risks. ABL is a commonly used financing tool in asset-heavy industries like manufacturing and distribution.

ABS (Asset-Backed Securities)

ABS are securities issued by securitizing various assets, such as loan receivables, leases, and installment payments, held by creditors. They are based on cash flows generated from assets like loan receivables, credit card debts, and auto loans, and sold to investors to raise capital. Through this process, issuers can convert assets into cash, while investors gain access to relatively stable cash flows. ABS are beneficial for dispersing asset risk and securing liquidity, making them a popular financing tool for companies and financial institutions. Investors can achieve stable and attractive returns through these securities, while issuers reduce debt and manage assets efficiently. ABS has become a diversified investment product in the financial market.

ADS (Alternative Depreciation System)

ADS is a method of calculating depreciation on assets over a more extended period, allowing slower depreciation expense recognition for tax purposes. It applies longer depreciation periods based on the asset's useful life, offering a more conservative approach than the standard MACRS (Modified Accelerated Cost Recovery System). U.S. tax law sometimes mandates ADS for specific assets or circumstances, such as assets used internationally or those receiving tax incentives. By gradually recognizing depreciation, ADS defers tax deductions and prevents excessive income reduction due to rapid depreciation. This method enables companies to allocate asset costs cautiously and more accurately reflect long-term asset use in financial performance.

ALM (Asset Liability Management)

ALM is a strategy used by companies and financial institutions to balance the maturity, yield, and risk of assets and liabilities to maintain financial stability and maximize returns. By aligning assets and liabilities, ALM effectively manages various financial risks, including interest rate changes, exchange rate fluctuations, and liquidity risks. This is particularly important for financial institutions, which adjust the profitability and risk of deposits (liabilities) and loans (assets) to secure liquidity and maximize returns. ALM plays a vital role in mitigating risks and maintaining a stable long-term financial structure. For instance, institutions manage the imbalance between long-term loans and short-term deposits to reduce risks from interest rate fluctuations. ALM strategies enhance a company's financial soundness and resilience, providing a solid foundation for financial management in uncertain market conditions.

AML (Anti-Money Laundering)

AML refers to regulations and procedures aimed at preventing and detecting money laundering, where illegal funds are concealed to appear legitimate within the financial system. It focuses on monitoring transaction records and reporting suspicious activities to prevent illicit funds from entering the economy. Key measures include the Know Your Customer (KYC) process and transaction monitoring systems, both essential for regulatory compliance in financial institutions. AML regulations play a crucial role in preventing criminal activities, such as terrorist financing, and maintaining transparency and trust in the financial system. Governments and international organizations are increasingly strengthening AML regulations, requiring financial institutions to manage money laundering risks effectively, which is vital for protecting institutional reputations and reducing legal risks.

AR (Annual Report)

The AR is an official document through which a company reports its financial performance, operational activities, and strategic accomplishments for the year to shareholders and stakeholders. It typically includes a message from management, financial statements (income statement, balance sheet, cash flow statement), key achievements, market analysis, and future strategies. This report enables shareholders to assess the company's financial health and operational results, providing essential information for investment decisions. The annual report enhances corporate transparency and credibility, fulfilling legal obligations. Public companies, in particular, are required to publish annual reports yearly under regulatory standards, conveying financial stability, risk management, and growth potential to shareholders and investors.

AS (Adverse Selection)

AS refers to a phenomenon where information asymmetry leads to the selection of lower-quality goods or services in the market. It frequently occurs in sectors like insurance, finance, and hiring, increasing the risk of poor decisions by the less-informed party (e.g., insurers, investors). For example, if an individual with poor health conceals their condition when purchasing insurance, the insurer may unknowingly accept a high-risk customer. Adverse selection reduces market efficiency and increases risk, prompting measures like mandatory disclosure and stricter screening processes. Insurers and financial institutions mitigate adverse selection by strengthening credit assessments and risk evaluations to address information asymmetry.

ASF (Available Stable Funding)

ASF is a metric representing the total amount of stable, long-term funding that a financial institution can rely on for asset operations. It primarily consists of low-volatility, long-maturity funds such as deposits, long-term loans, and capital, enabling financial institutions to continue operations during sudden liquidity crises. ASF plays a vital role in managing liquidity risk, and regulatory authorities include it in NSFR (Net Stable Funding Ratio) calculations to assess financial stability. By securing a diverse range of funding sources, ASF helps minimize risk and maintain long-term financial stability, enhancing an institution's resilience to external shocks, particularly in uncertain market environments.

BA (Banker's Acceptance)

BA is a bill guaranteed by a bank to enhance creditworthiness, commonly used as a financial instrument in international trade. By assuring payment on behalf of the issuer, the bank increases the bill's credibility, allowing companies to secure funds or provide payment guarantees to trading partners. Upon maturity, the bank fulfills the payment if the issuer cannot. BA plays a key role in short-term financing and international trade, often traded at a discount in the market. Leveraging the bank's credit, it enables low-cost funding, making BA valuable for corporate liquidity management and establishing trust in trade transactions.

BC (Block Chain)

BC is a decentralized data storage technology that records transaction data across multiple blocks and links them, creating a secure and tamper-resistant chain. Each block contains transaction information, which is then connected to previous blocks, ensuring high security against data manipulation. While initially used in cryptocurrency transactions like Bitcoin, block chain has recently been adopted in various industries such as finance, logistics, and healthcare as a reliable data management solution. By enabling participants to verify and manage data without a central authority, block chain enhances transparency and efficiency, reduces transaction costs, and facilitates rapid information sharing. Through automated processes like smart contracts, block chain can revolutionize business operations and is expected to play a key role in sectors requiring secure and transparent data management.

BCR (Benefit Cost Ratio)

BCR is a metric used to assess the economic feasibility of a project or investment by representing the ratio of expected benefits to total costs. A BCR greater than 1 indicates that benefits exceed costs, making the investment economically viable, while a BCR below 1 suggests inefficiency. This measure allows investors to easily compare the economic value a project offers. BCR is crucial in public infrastructure and environmental projects, aiding in optimal resource allocation. For instance, in public works like road construction, BCR analysis helps prioritize investments in projects with the highest economic benefits.

BE (Bandwagon Effect)

BE refers to the psychological phenomenon where individuals adopt choices or support opinions because they are popular or widely accepted by others. This effect often appears in consumption and behavior patterns, where more people align with certain products or views as they gain popularity. The bandwagon effect is prevalent in areas like fashion, politics, and media, driven by the mindset that "if many choose it, I should too." It significantly impacts consumer behavior, rapidly increasing product demand and spreading trends. Marketers leverage this effect by highlighting a product's popularity or showcasing positive reviews to encourage consumer purchases.

BE (Base Effect)

BE refers to a phenomenon where the rate of change in an indicator appears exaggerated or understated due to an unusually high or low baseline in the comparison period. Commonly seen in economic indicators like inflation or growth rates, it can distort the perceived economic situation when previous values were abnormally high or low. For instance, if last year's prices dropped sharply, the inflation rate in the following year may seem higher than the actual economic conditions reflect. The base effect is crucial to consider in economic analysis, helping to avoid over-interpretation by comparing long-term trends. This enables analysts to make more accurate economic judgments without relying heavily on temporary changes.

BEP (Break Even Point)

BEP is the point where a company's total revenue equals its total costs, meaning no profit or loss occurs. It is reached when total sales are sufficient to cover both fixed and variable costs. BEP helps companies set minimum revenue targets and forecast required sales volumes or revenue levels. This metric is crucial for understanding cost structures and developing strategies for pricing or cost reduction. For instance, sales exceeding the BEP generate profit, while sales below it results in losses. BEP analysis enables companies to create effective management plans and optimize resource allocation.

BIS (Bank for International Settlements)

BIS is an international financial organization established to promote cooperation among central banks and support financial stability. Acting as the central bank for central banks, BIS plays a vital role in maintaining global financial system stability. Headquartered in Basel, Switzerland, BIS conducts research on financial regulations and sets international standards, such as the Basel Accords, which establish guidelines for financial risk management and capital requirements. By preventing financial crises and facilitating information exchange among central banks, BIS bolsters global financial market stability.

BMS (Budgetary Management System)

BMS is a tool that organizations use to allocate financial resources efficiently and manage budgets systematically. It encompasses budget planning, approval, monitoring, and analysis processes, supporting the organization's financial planning and execution. BMS helps prevent budget overruns or waste, optimizing resource allocation for goal attainment. By tracking and analyzing financial status in realtime, BMS aids in financial decision-making and enhances cost efficiency. It compares actual spending against budgets, identifying trends of budget excesses early on. Particularly valuable in large organizations or public institutions, BMS ensures effective resource use and supports the achievement of financial objectives.

BOP (Balance of Payments)

BOP is a statistical record of all economic transactions between a country and the rest of the world over a specific period. It comprises three main accounts: the Current Account, Capital Account, and Financial Account, each divided by imports, exports, asset purchases, and sales. BOP serves as a critical indicator of a nation's external economic position, impacting foreign exchange reserves and exchange rate policies. It assesses the health of the national economy and helps maintain balance in international financial transactions. A current account deficit suggests high foreign dependency, while a surplus indicates strong export reliance or robust foreign capital inflow. BOP insights enable governments to adjust trade policies and economic strategies, ensuring economic stability.

BPS (Book-value per Share)

BPS represents the value of a company's net assets divided by its outstanding shares, providing insight into the asset value per share that shareholders hold. It is a key measure of financial stability, allowing investors to compare a company's intrinsic value with its current stock price. BPS indicates the asset value shareholders would theoretically receive if all assets were liquidated and liabilities settled. While stock prices fluctuate based on market expectations and demand, BPS reflects the book value of a company's actual assets. However, BPS only assesses asset value and does not account for future growth or profitability, and the book value may differ from actual market asset values. For example, assets with high book values may hold lower market valuations.

BR (Bank Run)

BR occurs when a widespread fear of a bank's potential failure leads many depositors to withdraw their funds simultaneously. During a bank run, the bank must handle large-scale withdrawal requests in a short time; if cash reserves are insufficient, it may face insolvency. Banks typically keep only a portion of deposits in cash, with the remainder invested or loaned out. Thus, if too many depositors demand withdrawals simultaneously, the bank may struggle to meet these demands immediately. Bank runs are usually triggered by economic instability, financial crises, or doubts about a bank's financial health, driven by depositors' urgency to secure funds before potential losses.

BS (Balance Sheet)

BS is a financial statement that presents a company's assets, liabilities, and equity at a specific point in time, offering a clear view of its financial standing. The asset section includes cash, property, and equipment, representing valuable resources owned, while liabilities cover debts such as bank loans and accounts payable. Equity, calculated as assets minus liabilities, reflects the ownership interest. The balance sheet ensures that the total assets equal the sum of liabilities and equity. This document is essential for evaluating a company's liquidity, financial stability, and debt levels, enabling investors and management to assess overall financial health and plan long-term strategies. It also provides key data on asset composition and debt maturity, crucial for anticipating financial risks.

BW (Bond with Warrant)

BW is a financial instrument combining a bond with an equity warrant, allowing investors to purchase the issuer's stock at a predetermined price within a specified period. This provides both bond interest income and the potential for additional profit if the stock price rises, making it an attractive option for investors. Consequently, issuers can secure funding at lower interest rates than standard bonds. BW enables investors to pursue both bond stability and stock growth potential, while issuers benefit from reduced funding costs and potential future equity issuance. Investors receive interest income until maturity and may convert to equity for added returns if the stock price appreciates. BW is often used by high-growth companies to attract investment, offering the flexibility of both stock and bond characteristics.

CAPEX (Capital Expenditure)

CAPEX refers to the costs incurred by a company to acquire or improve assets that will generate future revenue, primarily through long-term investments in physical assets like facilities, buildings, machinery, and equipment. CAPEX is a key metric for business growth and expansion, with spending reflected in financial statements, especially the cash flow statement and balance sheet. High CAPEX indicates a company's intent to expand physical assets for future revenue, while reduced CAPEX may suggest cutbacks in asset investment, potentially signaling slower growth. Unlike CAPEX, which pertains to long-term asset investment, OPEX (Operating Expenditure) covers daily operational costs such as salaries, rent, and raw materials necessary for immediate production and service provision.

CB (Circuit Breaker)

CB is a mechanism in financial markets designed to temporarily halt trading when stock prices experience extreme volatility, allowing investors a moment to regain composure and helping to moderate market fluctuations. This system is typically triggered by sudden, sharp declines or surges in stock prices, aiming to prevent panic selling or speculative buying due to excessive market volatility. Circuit breakers activate once prices move beyond a preset threshold, pausing trading momentarily. Developed primarily to prevent market crashes, circuit breakers reduce the chaos of mass sell-offs and are tailored differently across global exchanges. This system was introduced after the 1987 "Black Monday" market crash, where the New York Stock Exchange plummeted over 20% in one day, sparking global financial turmoil. By offering investors time for analysis, circuit breakers curb irrational trading during panics, enhancing market stability. However, temporary halts can also create confusion, and if panic persists post-breaker, additional volatility may ensue.

CB (Commercial Bank)

CB provides a range of financial services, including deposits, loans, and payment processing, to individuals and businesses. It allows customers to deposit funds, offers loans for various needs, and generates income from the interest spread between deposits and loans. Key services include checking accounts, credit card issuance, foreign exchange, and investment services. Commercial banks play a critical role in economic capital flow, supporting financial needs for businesses and individuals while contributing to financial stability. By offering loans, they support business growth and provide individuals with financing for housing, education, and more, all under central bank regulations to maintain credit supply, interest rates, and economic stability.

CB (Commercial Bill)

CB is a short-term financial instrument issued to settle trade debts between companies, primarily for the payment of goods or services. It typically has a short maturity and represents a commitment by a company to pay a specified amount at a future date. These bills can be discounted with financial institutions or transferred to other companies to enhance liquidity. As an essential tool for short-term financing, commercial bills help businesses manage cash flow from credit transactions and address temporary liquidity shortages. They can also be discounted or used as collateral, allowing companies to secure funds easily when needed.

CB (Convertible Bond)

CB is a bond that grants holders the right to convert the bond into the issuing company's stock under certain conditions. It combines features of both bonds and stocks, offering interest income along with the potential for capital gains through stock conversion. Investors can convert their bonds into shares if the stock price rises before maturity, achieving higher returns. Convertible bonds allow issuers to raise funds at lower interest rates and provide investors with additional profit opportunities if the stock appreciates. This instrument enables companies to secure favorable funding terms, while investors benefit from bond stability and stock growth potential. Convertible bonds are often used by high-growth companies for financing, offering investors a flexible investment option for risk management and profitability.

CB (Covered Bond)

CB is a bond secured by assets provided as collateral by the issuer, offering dual protection through the issuer's guarantee and the collateral pool. Typically backed by assets such as residential mortgages or public-sector loans, covered bonds ensure bondholders priority repayment from the collateral even if the issuer defaults. This structure makes covered bonds a highly secure investment. Widely used in Europe, covered bonds allow financial institutions to raise funds at relatively low interest rates while maintaining high credit quality. They provide institutions with stable funding, and investors benefit from low credit risk, making covered bonds an attractive investment option.

CBO (Collateralized Bond Obligation)

CBO is a financial product backed by a pool of bonds, often comprising lower-rated or high-yield bonds, which are bundled together and issued as collateralized securities. These are divided into multiple tranches, allowing investors to choose based on their risk preference, with the structure offering risk reduction through portfolio diversification. CBOs consolidate the cash flows from various bonds, spreading risk while potentially providing high returns, making them popular among institutional investors. However, returns are dependent on the performance of the underlying assets, so investors must carefully assess the credit risk and income structure of the underlying bonds.

CC (Credit Creation)

CC is the process by which banks expand the total money supply by lending out a portion of deposited funds, effectively creating new credit. Banks retain a fraction of deposits as reserves and use the remainder for loans, enabling each deposit to circulate multiple times through subsequent lending and depositing, thus amplifying credit within the economy. This mechanism supplies capital across the economy, promoting economic growth by supporting production and consumption. However, excessive credit creation can lead to inflation and financial instability, necessitating regulation and oversight by central banks to ensure sustainable economic growth.

CC (Credit Crunch)

CC occurs when banks and financial institutions reduce lending or tighten loan conditions, making it challenging to secure financing. Typically triggered by economic crises or financial system instability, a credit crunch can significantly impact the broader economy by restricting access to funds for businesses and individuals. If banks face asset quality issues or liquidity shortages, they become more cautious in lending, reducing the pool of eligible borrowers. During economic downturns, as repayment capacity declines, financial institutions cut back on lending to minimize risk. A credit crunch can decelerate economic activity, with businesses limiting investments and expansions and consumers reducing spending, potentially leading to prolonged economic stagnation. The 2008 global financial crisis is a notable example, where large-scale asset issues led banks to restrict lending. Central bank and government interventions are often required to alleviate credit crunches.

CCB (Contingent Convertible Bond)

CCB is a bond that converts to equity if specific conditions are met, primarily issued by financial institutions to strengthen their capital structure. When a bank fails to maintain capital adequacy, CCBs automatically convert to stock or, in some cases, are written down. This mechanism allows CCBs to serve as a loss-absorbing tool during financial crises, reinforcing the institution's capital base. By converting debt to equity, CCBs reduce liabilities and enhance capital, improving financial stability. In return for higher risk, CCBs typically offer higher interest rates than regular bonds, providing attractive returns to investors. However, investors face the risk of forced conversion to equity, potentially resulting in a loss of principal if the issuing bank's capital falls below a threshold. Due to this high-risk, high-reward profile, CCBs require thorough analysis from investors given their complex conditions and heightened likelihood of conversion under adverse market conditions.

CCF (Credit Conversion Factor)

CCF is a ratio used by financial institutions to estimate the credit risk associated with non-loan credit products (e.g., credit guarantees, credit card limits) that may potentially convert to actual loans. It predicts the probability that a portion of the provided credit will turn into actual lending, which is essential for calculating Risk-Weighted Assets (RWA) under Basel III regulations. CCF reflects the likelihood of non-loan exposures transitioning to loans, influencing capital requirements. For instance, a credit card limit might have a CCF of 20%, indicating a 20% probability of the credit limit becoming an actual loan. Depending on the product's nature, CCF typically ranges from 0% to 100%, with certain guarantees potentially set at 100%.

CCP (Central Counter Party)

CCP acts as an intermediary in financial transactions, standing between buyers and sellers to ensure smooth trading and reduce settlement risk. In each transaction, the CCP assumes the role of buyer to the seller and seller to the buyer, guaranteeing the completion of trades for assets such as derivatives, stocks, and bonds, thereby enhancing market stability and reliability. By centralizing and managing trade clearances, CCPs mitigate counterparty credit risk; if one party defaults, the CCP steps in to fulfill the obligation. To manage potential losses, CCPs require margin deposits from each party, providing a buffer against risks within trades. By reducing uncertainty, simplifying processes, and promoting transparency, CCPs lower transaction costs, accelerate processing, and diminish systemic credit risk, preventing risk transmission across the financial system.

CCSI (Composite Consumer Sentiment Index)

CCSI quantifies consumer perceptions of the current and future economic outlook. It evaluates consumer expectations and confidence related to economic activities through surveys on household spending capacity, employment status, and cost of living. A high CCSI indicates a positive consumer outlook and a likelihood of increased spending, while a low CCSI suggests economic uncertainty and a tendency to reduce spending. CCSI is a crucial indicator for predicting consumption trends and monitoring economic fluctuations. Policymakers and businesses use CCSI insights to gauge consumer sentiment, informing economic policies and business strategies.

CD (Certificate of Deposit)

CD is a financial product in which a fixed amount is deposited for a set period, with the principal and interest returned at maturity. It is transferable, allowing the depositor to transfer ownership to others, a feature distinguishing it from regular deposits, and is actively traded in short-term financial markets. CDs typically have terms of 3 months, 6 months, or 1 year, during which withdrawals are not allowed. Upon maturity, the depositor receives the principal and the agreed-upon interest. This transferability enhances CD liquidity, making it advantageous for corporate cash management. CDs offer a fixed interest rate that varies according to the market rate and economic conditions at issuance.

CD (Countervailing Duties)

CD is a tariff imposed by an importing country to offset the effects of subsidies provided by an exporting country, which artificially boost its products' competitiveness. This duty acts as a protective trade measure to prevent harm to domestic industries or market distortion due to subsidized exports. Countervailing duties are typically enforced under WTO guidelines; if an exporting country subsidizes its products to lower export prices, the importing country may levy a countervailing duty to neutralize the subsidy's impact and maintain fair competition. To impose this duty, the importing country must investigate and substantiate the subsidy and resultant harm to its industries, analyzing the export country's subsidy policies and the domestic industry's impact. Once approved, an additional tariff is applied to the subsidized goods. While countervailing duties protect local industries, they can raise import prices for consumers and risk trade conflicts, necessitating careful compliance with international procedures.

CD (Credit Derivative)

CD is a financial instrument designed to trade credit risk, enabling investors and institutions to manage the credit risk associated with assets like bonds and loans issued by corporations, governments, or financial institutions. This product allows parties to transfer the risk of default on specific credit assets to third parties, offering a way for institutions to retain assets while mitigating associated risks. Credit derivatives are commonly used by financial institutions to hedge against potential credit losses on bonds or loans, transferring this risk in exchange for a premium. For instance, if a bank anticipates a borrower's risk of default, it may use a CDS (Credit Default Swap) to transfer that risk to a third party, paying a premium for the coverage.

CDO (Collateralized Debt Obligation)

CDO is a derivative financial product backed by a pool of various financial assets, such as bonds and loans, structured to spread risk and raise funds. Financial institutions bundle these assets and categorize them into "tranches," which are then sold to investors. Each tranche varies in risk and return, with higher tranches offering lower risk and yields, and lower tranches carrying higher risk but potentially greater returns. CDOs allow investors to select investments matching their risk tolerance while enabling institutions to transfer loan risks and secure additional funding. However, due to their complexity and difficulty in risk assessment, CDOs were pivotal in the 2008 financial crisis. High-risk CDOs, including subprime mortgages, resulted in massive defaults and significant losses for investors.

CEA (Credit Equivalent Amount)

CEA represents the assessed credit risk amount in financial institutions for derivative or credit-related transactions. It adjusts for potential market value fluctuations and credit risks within derivatives, converting these risks into an equivalent amount comparable to loans or bonds. Primarily used by financial institutions for risk management and capital adequacy, CEA enables more precise loss estimation in transactions. It is calculated for outstanding derivative contracts by assessing market value and potential credit exposure, providing a risk-aligned amount in line with Basel capital requirements. CEA is essential for financial institutions to evaluate and manage the credit risk embedded in derivatives and non-loan credit transactions, ensuring adequate capital reserves to counter counterparty default risk.

CET1 (Common Equity Tier 1)

CET1 is the core capital ratio that measures a bank's financial soundness, considering the quality and risk of capital. Composed of high-quality capital like common equity and retained earnings, CET1 helps banks absorb losses and maintain stability during financial crises. Under BIS standards, a higher CET1 ratio indicates a more robust financial structure. The ratio is calculated as CET1 capital divided by risk-weighted assets, and banks must meet a regulatory minimum to ensure resilience. Since CET1 reflects a bank's capacity to withstand losses, it plays a crucial role in risk management and stability. If the CET1 ratio falls, banks may raise additional capital or manage assets to restore the required level.

CF (Crowd Funding)

CF is a fundraising method where funds are collected from a large number of individuals, typically through online platforms, to support specific projects, businesses, or ideas. Unlike traditional financing, individuals or companies raise funds by recruiting investors or donors directly via platforms. It's popular for funding innovative ideas and startups, offering various rewards or incentives to backers. Crowdfunding is classified as follows:

1) Reward-based: Backers receive non-monetary rewards, such as products or services, upon project success.
2) Donation-based: Contributions are made purely out of goodwill, with no financial return expected, often for nonprofits or social projects.
3) Equity-based: Investors provide funds in exchange for equity or profit shares, commonly used by startups.
4) Loan-based: Funds are provided as loans, with repayment plus interest over time, often used by small businesses.

CFC (Common Fund for Commodities)

CFC is an international financial institution established by the United Nations (UN) and UNCTAD to support and promote commodity production and trade in developing countries. It primarily funds development projects in sectors such as agriculture, mining, and energy, aiming to foster economic growth and poverty reduction in these regions. CFC's core goal is to help developing nations manage their natural resources and commodities more effectively, contributing to economic self-reliance. The fund enhances production capacity, supports infrastructure and technological innovation in commodity industries, and expands market access to boost exports, thereby helping developing countries secure a stronger position in the global economy.

CFS (Cash Flow Statement)

CFS is a financial statement that records a company's cash inflows and outflows over a specific period, showing how cash is generated, used, and managed. It is essential for assessing financial health, systematically categorizing cash movements from operating, investing, and financing activities. The CFS allows for evaluating cash management efficiency and liquidity, highlighting any potential cash shortages that could impact operations despite profitability. As a critical indicator of sustainability, the CFS provides insights into a company's ability to maintain sufficient cash for ongoing activities and future obligations.

CI (Composite Indexes of Business Indicators)

CI is a statistical indicator that combines multiple economic metrics to assess the overall state of the economy and predict future trends. It is categorized into leading, coincident, and lagging indices, each reflecting different aspects of economic activity. CI is a crucial tool for policymakers, investors, and economists, providing a comprehensive analysis of economic cycles and aiding in forecasts of growth, recession, or recovery. Components of CI include:
1) Leading Index: Predicts future economic changes and includes indicators like the stock market, building permits, and consumer sentiment, which typically change before the economy shifts.

2) Coincident Index: Reflects the current economic state, including metrics like industrial production, employment, and retail sales.
3) Lagging Index: Responds after economic shifts, featuring indicators like unemployment rates and corporate debt, helping to confirm and evaluate changes.

CIA (Certified Internal Auditor)

CIA is an internationally recognized certification in the audit field, validating expertise in internal auditing. Issued by the IIA (Institute of Internal Auditors) in the United States, this certification affirms proficiency in conducting internal audits, risk management, control, governance, and evaluating management processes. It is a key credential for professionals aiming to establish credibility in the internal audit profession.

CL (Credit Leverage)

CL is a financial strategy that uses borrowed funds to expand investment size or acquire assets, thereby aiming to increase returns. It enables investors to manage assets larger than their capital, commonly applied in real estate, stocks, and derivatives. While successful leverage can yield high returns on capital, it also amplifies potential losses during market downturns. Credit leverage enhances capital efficiency and maximizes investment performance, frequently used by financial institutions and large investors. However, excessive leverage can lead to financial instability, prompting regulatory authorities to enforce leverage ratio limits to strengthen risk management.

CLN (Credit Linked Notes)

CLN is a derivative financial instrument that links credit risk to a specific asset, allowing investors to earn interest by assuming the credit risk associated with a particular entity or asset. Typically combined with a Credit Default Swap (CDS), CLNs operate such that investors gain or lose based on the credit status of the underlying asset, often bonds or loans. Investors provide capital to the issuer and receive interest if the asset avoids default; however, in the event of default, they may lose part or all of their principal. For instance, if a CLN is linked to a company's credit risk, investors face losses if that company defaults. CLNs offer high-interest rates, providing opportunities for attractive returns while enabling risk diversification across assets. Due to their complex structure and inherent credit and derivative risks, investors must thoroughly understand CLNs to avoid underestimating potential risks.

CLO (Collateralized Loan Obligation)

CLO is a derivative financial product backed by a pool of loans, primarily corporate loans, structured to provide investors with returns based on interest and principal repayments from the underlying loans. CLOs bundle multiple loans and issue securities in tranches, each offering different levels of risk and return. Senior tranches are safer with lower yields, while junior tranches take on higher risk for potentially greater returns. This structure allows investors to choose investments matching their risk tolerance. However, if the repayment capability of the underlying corporate loans deteriorates or market instability rises, CLOs can lead to investor losses.

CM (Capital Market)

CM is a financial market for long-term funding and asset trading, primarily involving stocks and bonds. It serves as a platform for companies, governments, and individuals to raise long-term capital and earn investment returns, divided into stock and bond markets.

Through capital markets, corporations and governments secure substantial funding, while investors gain opportunities for capital returns, supporting economic growth by facilitating financial flows. An efficient capital market provides diversification for investors and encourages fund inflows, enabling stable funding for entities and long-term investment in growth-oriented assets for investors.

CMA (Cash Management Account)

CMA is a comprehensive financial account that combines cash management and asset investment features, offered mainly by banks and brokerage firms. Beyond simply holding cash, it integrates services like deposits, interest earnings, and investment management, enhancing liquidity and facilitating efficient short-term asset management for individuals and businesses. CMAs allow easy cash deposits and withdrawals, aiding in effective fund management. Like a bank account, they may pay interest on deposited funds, and some CMAs offer higher rates through investment-linked options. Additionally, CMAs are often linked with brokerage accounts, enabling convenient access to investments in assets like stocks and bonds.

CMO (Collateralized Mortgage Obligation)

CMO is a derivative financial product backed by a pool of mortgage loans, specifically residential mortgages. These loans are bundled and securitized, then divided into multiple tranches, each offering distinct levels of risk and return, allowing investors to choose based on their risk tolerance. CMOs distribute the principal and interest payments from the underlying mortgages among investors according to tranche priority. Higher tranches provide more stable cash flows, while lower tranches carry higher risk but offer the potential for higher returns. By securitizing mortgages, CMOs help financial institutions recover funds for reinvestment, while offering investors options for risk management and portfolio diversification. However, CMO values are sensitive to factors like interest rate changes, housing market instability, and borrower defaults. During the 2008 financial crisis, CMOs linked to subprime mortgages suffered significant losses.

CMS (Cash Management Service)

CMS is a financial service designed to help companies manage cash flow efficiently, optimizing liquidity and offering comprehensive solutions like receivables, payables management, and asset handling. CMS enables companies to streamline cash operations, reduce operational costs, and enhance profitability by overseeing cash inflows and outflows, payments, and payroll systematically, ensuring funds are available when needed. It provides real-time monitoring and reporting, allowing management to easily assess financial health and make informed decisions. Additionally, CMS facilitates short-term investment of surplus cash for extra returns and automates cash flow processes, reducing labor costs and operational expenses. With transparent cash flow tracking, CMS enhances resource allocation, helping companies run an efficient financial structure.

CMS (Credit Management System)

CMS is a tool used by companies and financial institutions to manage credit risk and make informed credit-related decisions. It aids in assessing customer creditworthiness, setting appropriate credit limits, and managing loan approvals and collections systematically. CMS optimizes risk management by analyzing customer credit history, financial status, and repayment records to evaluate credit risk, allowing institutions to set suitable credit limits. It also offers loan management functions, including repayment scheduling, interest calculations, and delinquency tracking. By managing overdue accounts and initiating collections when needed, CMS helps reduce bad debt ratios and mitigate risks. Through precise credit analysis, CMS predicts default probabilities, limits high-risk transactions, and automates credit evaluation, enabling swift and accurate decision-making while maintaining transparency in cash flow and debt status.

CO (Call Option)

A CO is a type of derivative contract that grants the buyer the right, but not the obligation, to purchase an underlying asset at a specified price (strike price) on or before a future date. The buyer can choose not to exercise the option if market conditions are unfavorable. Commonly used with assets like stocks, bonds, and commodities, call options allow investors to bet on price increases. The buyer benefits if the asset's market price exceeds the strike price, while the seller must sell the asset at the strike price if the option is exercised. Call options are categorized as European (exercisable only at expiration) or American (exercisable any time before expiration). Investors use call options to limit risk while capturing potential gains from asset price increases, and holders of underlying assets can sell call options to earn additional income.

COFIX (Cost of Funds Index)

COFIX is an index that reflects the cost banks incur to raise funds, serving as a key benchmark for setting variable mortgage rates in South Korea. It aggregates the costs of funds raised through deposits, savings, and bonds, reflecting the funding environment in the financial market. Calculated based on the funding costs of eight major Korean banks, COFIX is published monthly on the 15th and directly influences variable-rate mortgage interest rates. When funding costs rise, mortgage rates increase, and vice versa, providing transparency and reducing volatility in loan rates. COFIX enables loan rates to align realistically with actual funding costs, enhancing predictability for both borrowers and financial institutions. However, as COFIX is based on the previous month's costs, it may not fully capture real-time market conditions, potentially leading to unexpected rate fluctuations for borrowers.

COGS (Cost of Goods Sold)

COGS represents the direct costs incurred in producing goods or services, essential for calculating gross profit. It includes expenses like raw materials, direct labor, and manufacturing overhead, excluding indirect and operating costs. Subtracting COGS from sales revenue yields gross profit, crucial for assessing production efficiency. COGS provides insight into cost structure and production efficiency, aiding in pricing strategy and profit margin analysis. Lower COGS indicates higher profitability, reflecting efficient resource management, while high COGS can reduce margins, impacting profitability.

CP (Capital Productivity)

CP is an indicator measuring how efficiently a company or entire economy utilizes invested capital to produce output. Calculated as the ratio of output to capital input, it assesses the ability to maximize production from capital investment, playing a vital role in analyzing economic growth, investment efficiency, and corporate profitability. A higher capital productivity indicates greater output per unit of capital, enhancing profitability and optimizing resource allocation. While CP is valuable for evaluating capital efficiency, it is also influenced by other factors such as labor productivity and technological advancements, so a comprehensive assessment should consider these additional elements. Ultimately, understanding capital productivity is essential for making informed investment decisions and driving sustainable growth.

CP (Commercial Paper)

CP is an unsecured short-term debt instrument used by corporations to quickly raise funds, typically with maturities under 90 days. It is primarily issued by creditworthy companies to meet operating expenses or cover temporary cash flow needs, with a maximum maturity of 270 days, though commonly issued for 30 to 90 days. As an unsecured instrument, investor confidence in CP depends on the issuing company's credit rating, favoring high-credit firms for favorable rates. CP is issued at a discount to face value, with interest realized as the difference upon maturity. It's a popular tool for covering short-term needs like payroll or inventory purchases.

CP (Contractionary Policy)

CP refers to fiscal and monetary measures implemented by governments or central banks to curb economic overheating and inflation. To slow economic activity and control price increases, methods like raising taxes, reducing government spending, and increasing interest rates are employed. The primary goal of contractionary policy is to stabilize the economy by controlling inflation and preventing overheating. It is typically used when prices surge or financial instability threatens. Key tools include monetary policy—raising interest rates to increase borrowing costs and reduce spending and investment—and fiscal policy, such as tax hikes and reduced government expenditure to decrease available market funds. While contractionary policy helps control inflation and maintain economic balance, excessive tightening can lead to slower growth and higher unemployment.

CPA (Certified Public Accountant)

CPA is a certified accounting professional with expertise in areas such as accounting, tax, auditing, and financial management. CPAs perform tasks like preparing financial statements, filing taxes, conducting audits, and analyzing finances, managing and improving the financial health of businesses and individuals. This credential verifies a high level of professionalism and is trusted by corporations and government agencies for advisory roles. CPAs ensure compliance with accounting and tax regulations and guarantee financial reporting accuracy. They also assist companies in addressing complex accounting issues, developing tax-saving strategies, and enhancing financial stability. CPA certification is recognized as a prestigious qualification demanding credibility and expertise in the accounting and finance sectors.

CPI (Consumer Price Index)

CPI is a key indicator that measures the average price changes over time for goods and services purchased by consumers, used primarily to assess inflation. Calculated from price variations in essential items like food, housing, healthcare, and other household needs, CPI reflects the rise or fall in price levels within an economy and indicates shifts in consumer purchasing power. It serves as a critical benchmark in economic policymaking, wage adjustments, pension increases, and welfare programs to maintain real living standards. Central banks use CPI to guide interest rate policies, aiming to control inflation and stabilize the economy. CPI trends are essential for businesses, policymakers, and individuals in making informed economic decisions.

CPI (Cost-Push Inflation)

CPI refers to an economic phenomenon where the prices of goods and services rise due to increased production costs, such as higher raw material prices, wage increases, and energy costs. This type of inflation occurs when these rising costs drive up final consumer prices, even without an increase in demand, primarily triggered by supply-side factors. Cost-push inflation can lead to reduced supply and a decline in real purchasing power, often accompanying economic slowdowns and potentially stalling growth. When it occurs, companies may reduce output or raise prices to manage costs, impacting consumer purchasing power and profitability negatively. To control cost-push inflation, governments may use monetary policies, such as raising interest rates, to mitigate inflationary pressures.

CR (Capitalization Rate)

CR, also known as Cap Rate, is a metric used to assess the return on investment (ROI) in real estate. It is calculated by dividing the net operating income from a property by its market value, reflecting the annual rate of return an investor can expect. A high cap rate indicates greater potential returns (and possibly higher risk), while a low cap rate suggests a more stable investment with lower returns. The cap rate helps investors determine if a property is overvalued or undervalued relative to the market average. Investors use the cap rate based on their risk tolerance to make informed investment decisions.

CRAs (Credit Ratings Agencies)

CRAs assess the credit risk of entities such as corporations, governments, or financial products and assign credit ratings accordingly. These agencies analyze an issuer's ability and willingness to meet debt obligations, providing investors with reliable information to make informed decisions. Leading CRAs include Moody's, S&P Global, and Fitch. By evaluating the creditworthiness of bonds or financial instruments, CRAs help predict default probabilities, guiding investment choices. Lower ratings indicate higher risk, potentially leading to higher borrowing costs or investor aversion, while higher ratings signify safety, allowing for lower borrowing costs. CRAs play a crucial role in financial markets but have faced criticism for rating inaccuracies, notably during the 2008 financial crisis when they incorrectly rated subprime mortgage-linked products.

CS (Credit Spread)

CS is the yield difference between a risky asset and a risk-free asset, typically seen between corporate bonds and government bonds. This spread reflects the additional return investors demand as compensation for the credit risk that a company or issuer might default. Calculated by subtracting the risk-free rate (often a government bond yield) from a corporate bond's yield, the credit spread varies with the bond's credit risk. Lower credit ratings lead to higher spreads, indicating that investors require greater returns for higher risk. For instance, investment-grade bonds have smaller spreads, while junk bonds (speculative-grade) have larger spreads due to higher risk. Credit spreads also fluctuate with economic conditions, widening in uncertain or unstable markets as credit risk rises, and narrowing in stable environments, allowing cheaper corporate funding.

CSD (Central Securities Depository)

A CSD is an institution responsible for the secure storage and settlement of securities such as stocks and bonds. It manages ownership records digitally, playing a critical role in post-trade settlement processes. By holding securities in physical or electronic form, CSDs safeguard ownership rights and facilitate the transfer of securities to buyers and payments to sellers, ensuring automated and transparent settlement. Through accurate record-keeping, CSDs reflect ownership changes following trades, enhancing market efficiency and reducing risks. This allows investors to minimize complexities and costs in securities management, promoting stability and security within financial markets.

CSI (Consumer Survey Index)

CSI quantifies consumer perceptions of the current economic climate and expectations for the future. Reflecting consumer confidence in both present conditions and future economic prospects, CSI is a valuable tool for economic policy formulation and forecasting. It includes evaluations of current and anticipated living standards and captures plans for big-ticket purchases like appliances, cars, and homes. Since CSI gauges consumer sentiment, it is useful for predicting economic trends; a high CSI suggests increased consumer spending and potential economic growth, whereas a low CSI indicates potential consumption restraint and economic slowdown.

CSS (Credit Scoring System)

CSS is a scoring mechanism used by financial institutions to assess an individual's creditworthiness, helping predict repayment ability and credit risk. It evaluates credit scores based on factors like financial transaction history, credit card usage, loan repayment records, and income. This score guides institutions in making loan approval decisions, setting interest rates, and managing risk. CSS supports efficient credit assessment, reducing lending risk and enabling faster decision-making, allowing high-credit individuals to secure favorable loan terms. It is a vital tool in the financial sector for risk management and loan strategy development.

CWM (Chain Weighted Method)

CWM is a calculation approach used to measure price indices or economic growth rates. It reflects annual changes in prices and quantities, providing a more accurate assessment of economic performance without being fixed to a base year's price structure. By updating price weights each year, CWM captures changes in both product prices and consumer consumption patterns, effectively incorporating substitution effects between goods. This method helps avoid distortions that can occur with fixed-weight methods, which may be influenced by the price structure of a specific year. CWM is commonly applied in GDP calculations and price indices, making it useful for comparing multiple years. It accurately reflects consumers' changing consumption patterns and price fluctuations, allowing for a better measurement of economic growth and inflation by renewing weights annually to represent current economic conditions.

D&A (Depreciation and Amortization)

D&A is the accounting method used to reflect the reduction in value of tangible assets (depreciation) and intangible assets (amortization) over time. It indicates how assets lose value as they are used, allowing businesses to gradually expense the asset's cost over its useful life. Both depreciation and amortization are crucial components of a company's financial statements, significantly impacting net income and cash flow. By distributing the cost of an asset over its lifespan instead of expensing it all at once, companies can provide a more accurate reflection of profitability. Furthermore, D&A protects cash flow, as these are accounting expenses rather than actual cash outflows.

DCB (Dual Currency Bond)

DCB refers to a bond issued and redeemed in two different currencies. Typically, the principal and interest are paid in different currencies, making this type of bond appealing to investors and companies' sensitive to exchange rate fluctuations when raising funds or investing in capital markets. For instance, a bond might be issued with its principal in one currency (e.g., US dollars) while the interest is paid in another (e.g., euros or yen). Investors receive interest payments based on a predetermined rate in the specified currency, while the principal is repaid in the currency in which it was originally issued. DCBs allow investors to simultaneously manage exchange rate risks and opportunities. For example, if the principal is received in dollars and interest in yen, an increase in the yen's value at the time of interest payment could yield additional profits. Conversely, adverse exchange rate movements could lead to losses. Companies holding assets and liabilities in multiple currencies may issue dual currency bonds to hedge against currency risks. Additionally, investors with diversified international portfolios may utilize DCBs to generate returns in various currencies. However, DCBs are significantly impacted by exchange rate volatility, requiring investors to be aware of the potential for both high returns and high risks.

DDM (Dividend Discount Model)

DDM is a method for valuing a stock by discounting future expected dividends to their present value. This model assumes that a stock's value is determined by the present value of the dividends it will pay in the future. Since the stock price is based on dividends, DDM is particularly useful for evaluating companies with stable dividend policies. The model estimates stock price using the dividend growth rate and discount rate, allowing for various scenarios through fixed growth models or multi-stage growth models. This approach helps investors assess whether a stock is overvalued or undervalued based on its current price, aiding in the formulation of long-term investment strategies. DDM is an effective evaluation tool for stocks expected to generate stable cash flows. This model provides a structured framework for investors to make informed decisions about their investments in dividend-paying stocks.

DE (Demonstration Effect)

DE refers to the phenomenon where the consumption behaviors of one social group or individual influence the consumption patterns of others. It illustrates the tendency for individuals to adjust their spending based on the observed consumption habits of those around them. This concept is significant in both economics and sociology, profoundly impacting personal and collective economic decisions. The demonstration effect is driven by the psychological inclination to imitate others' spending behaviors, often regardless of one's income level. For instance, lower-income individuals might attempt to mimic the consumption styles of higher-income individuals. This effect can stimulate consumer tendencies, leading to increased overall consumption and contributing to economic growth. However, it may also encourage individuals with insufficient income to engage in excessive spending, exacerbating income inequality and increasing debt levels. The demonstration effect is especially pronounced through advertising, media, and social networks, exemplified by trends where consumers follow the product choices of celebrities or influencers on social media.

DF (Direct Financing)

DF refers to the method by which companies or governments raise capital directly from investors without the intermediation of financial institutions. This involves issuing securities such as stocks or bonds to attract funds from investors, contrasting with indirect financing, where funds are borrowed through financial intermediaries. In direct financing, the issuing entity engages with investors through the securities market, minimizing or eliminating the role of intermediaries, allowing funds to flow directly from investors to the issuer. This approach helps reduce transaction costs, as there are no intermediary fees. Companies can raise substantial amounts of capital at once, accessing a broad range of investors via stock or bond markets. However, because investors provide funds directly, the issuer's credit risk is directly transferred to them. Issuing stocks or bonds involves legal processes and regulatory compliance, which can require extensive procedures.

DLT (Distributed Ledger Technology)

DLT is a system that enables multiple participants to share and simultaneously update the same ledger across a distributed network without a centralized server. By storing data across multiple nodes (participants) rather than a single central server, DLT ensures data transparency, security, and integrity. A prominent example of DLT is block chain, which allows transaction records to be distributed and securely stored. In DLT, all participants maintain identical copies of the data, and any new transactions are simultaneously updated across the network. This decentralized approach helps maintain data accuracy and reliability without a central authority, significantly reducing the risks of data tampering or hacking. DLT is widely utilized in various fields, including finance, supply chain management, asset trading, and government record management. It plays a crucial role in cryptocurrencies (e.g., Bitcoin) and contributes to automating payments and contract execution within financial systems.

DPI (Demand-Pull Inflation)

DPI is an economic concept that describes the phenomenon where overall demand exceeds total supply, leading to rising prices. It occurs when demand increases rapidly, and businesses are unable to sufficiently supply goods and services to meet that demand. This situation contributes to inflationary pressure in the economy. DPI typically arises during periods of economic growth and rising employment, as consumers seek to purchase more products and services. For example, government expansionary fiscal policies that inject funds into the market can boost demand, while central banks lowering interest rates can further stimulate consumption and investment, increasing demand even more. When demand surges in a limited supply environment, companies tend to raise prices, resulting in inflation. While moderate demand increases can promote economic growth, excessive demand-pull inflation can negatively impact the economy in the long term.

DPI (Disposable Personal Income)

DPI represents the amount of income that individuals can actually spend or save after taxes and social security contributions have been deducted. It reflects the net income available for personal expenses, consumption, savings, and investments, serving as a crucial indicator of an individual or household's economic health. DPI is calculated by subtracting taxes (primarily income tax) and social security contributions from total income, indicating the residual income left after mandatory expenditures. A higher DPI allows consumers to spend or save more, significantly stimulating economic activity. DPI is an important metric for analyzing economic conditions, as it helps assess consumer spending and savings rates. An increase in disposable income can promote economic growth, while a decrease may lead to reduced consumption and heighten the risk of economic recession.

DPL (Deposit Placement Line)

DPL refers to the maximum amount that financial institutions set for clients when investing or holding funds in specific deposit products. It establishes the ceiling on the deposits that a bank can accept from customers or the upper limit for a particular deposit product. This limit serves as an important tool for liquidity management and risk management, forming part of the asset and liability management strategy of financial institutions. By setting deposit limits, institutions can prevent excessive inflows of funds and facilitate optimal management of customer deposits while diversifying risk. Specific deposit products may have defined maximum amounts based on interest rates or terms, helping to minimize liquidity risk. Deposit limits enable financial institutions to effectively manage liquidity by avoiding an overwhelming concentration of deposits in one area, which can lead to associated risks, thereby enhancing overall stability.

DR (Depositary Receipts)

DR is a financial instrument that allows investors in one country to indirectly invest in foreign stocks without directly purchasing them. These receipts are issued to facilitate trading of foreign company shares in the local currency. A depositary bank holds the shares of a foreign company and issues corresponding depositary receipts to local investors. This enables investors to trade these receipts on their domestic financial markets, thereby increasing accessibility to foreign investments. Since DRs are denominated in the local currency and are subject to local laws, they help mitigate foreign exchange risk and simplify legal processes. This mechanism enhances the ability of investors to participate in international markets while maintaining the convenience of domestic trading.

DSCR (Debt Service Coverage Ratio)

DSCR is an indicator that measures a company's or individual's ability to cover debt repayments with their operating income. It serves as a critical metric for creditors and investors to assess the financial health and debt repayment capacity of an entity. DSCR is calculated by dividing operating income (typically EBITDA) by the debt service amount, which includes both interest and principal repayments due during the period. A DSCR greater than 1 indicates that operating income exceeds the debt service obligations, signifying sufficient financial capacity to repay debts. Conversely, a DSCR of 1 or less suggests that operating income may not be sufficient to cover debt repayments, raising concerns about the entity's ability to meet its financial obligations.

DSR (Debt Service Ratio)

DSR is an indicator that measures the ratio of an individual's or company's annual income to their debt repayment obligations, including both principal and interest. It is used to evaluate how efficiently a borrower can repay their debts based on their income over a specified period. DSR plays a crucial role in loan assessments and financial evaluations, serving as a key criterion for measuring a debtor's repayment capacity. The DSR is calculated by dividing the total debt repayment amount by total income and converting it into a percentage. Here, the total debt repayment amount includes both the principal and interest of loans, while total income typically refers to the annual earnings of the individual or entity. A lower DSR indicates that a smaller portion of income is dedicated to debt repayment, suggesting less financial burden and lower credit risk in the eyes of financial institutions. Conversely, a higher DSR implies that a significant portion of income is allocated to servicing debt, potentially indicating repayment difficulties and making it harder to secure additional loans.

DTI (Debt to Income Ratio)

DTI is an indicator that measures the proportion of an individual's debt repayment obligations relative to their income. It serves as a crucial criterion for financial institutions when assessing a loan applicant's repayment ability. The DTI ratio indicates what percentage of monthly income is allocated to debt repayments, with a higher percentage signifying a greater debt burden. DTI is calculated by dividing the total monthly debt repayments by the monthly income and expressing it as a percentage. Monthly debt repayments include all obligations, such as mortgage payments, credit card bills, and auto loans, while monthly income refers to the individual's after-tax earnings. A lower DTI ratio indicates that the individual has less debt relative to their income, suggesting higher repayment capacity and increasing the likelihood of loan approval. Conversely, a higher DTI ratio implies a heavier debt burden relative to income, indicating potential difficulties in repaying loans, which may lead to loan application rejections.

DVP (Delivery versus Payment)

DVP is a settlement method in which the delivery of securities and the payment for those securities occur simultaneously. This approach is designed to minimize risks associated with securities transactions, ensuring that both the transfer of securities and the payment are conditional; if one side is not completed, the entire transaction is not executed. DVP significantly reduces settlement risk, ensuring that both the securities and the payment are exchanged securely. Primarily used in securities trading, DVP is facilitated by central securities depositories (CSDs) or settlement banks to ensure safe execution of large financial transactions. This method applies not only to stocks and bonds but also to derivatives, enhancing transaction security. Under the DVP system, the securities settlement mechanism retains both the securities and funds until the transaction is finalized, with immediate payment occurring upon the delivery of the securities. This means that the receiving party only receives the securities when they make the payment, effectively preventing settlement failures. Since funds are not disbursed until the securities are delivered, the risks of payment default or non-delivery of securities are significantly reduced. This arrangement minimizes the risk for both parties involved in the transaction, as each side fulfills its payment obligations securely.

EAD (Exposure at Default)

EAD refers to the amount of assets that a financial institution cannot recover when a borrower defaults. It is a critical metric in credit risk management, used to estimate the potential loss that a financial institution may incur from loans or credit transactions in the event of default. By predicting the potential losses associated with default, EAD plays an essential role in helping financial institutions establish capital reserves and risk management strategies. EAD is calculated based on the outstanding amount at the time of default, including both the loan balance and any unused portions of credit limits, such as credit cards. For instance, if a borrower defaults, the financial institution considers not only the remaining loan amount but also any available credit that could be drawn upon, thus determining the exposure amount. EAD is a vital component of international financial regulations, such as Basel II and Basel III, which ensure that financial institutions maintain adequate capital to mitigate credit risk. By forecasting potential losses, EAD contributes to the financial stability of institutions, enabling them to manage liabilities effectively and set aside sufficient capital reserves. Financial institutions utilize EAD to make loss predictions considering a borrower's likelihood of default, which aids in developing debt management strategies and allocating capital reserves appropriately.

EB (Exchangeable Bond)

EB is a type of bond that provides the issuing company with the option to exchange it for shares of another company that it owns. Before the bond's maturity, the bondholder has the right, under certain conditions, to exchange the bond for shares of a different company, making it an attractive product for investors anticipating an increase in stock prices. While similar to convertible bonds (CBs), which can be converted into shares of the issuing company, exchangeable bonds differ in that they can be converted into shares of a different company. In the case of EB, the bondholder holds the right to exchange their bond for shares of another company owned by the issuing firm. Investors can benefit from potential stock price appreciation while also receiving interest payments during the holding period. If the stock price rises, bondholders can gain profit through the exchange. Beyond the possibility of stock exchange, bondholders can also receive principal repayment at maturity or continue to earn interest, providing a stable investment option. Exchangeable bonds are particularly appealing to investors looking to capitalize on potential stock price increases while allowing companies to raise capital effectively. By issuing exchangeable bonds, companies can secure funding while offering investors the opportunity to benefit from equity appreciation.

EBITDA (Earnings Before Interest, Tax, Depreciation, and Amortization)

EBITDA is a financial metric that reflects a company's operating income by excluding interest, taxes, depreciation, and amortization. It is used to evaluate the cash flows generated from a company's core operating activities, providing insights into its profitability and operational efficiency. EBITDA is particularly useful for assessing a company's financial performance, as it focuses on earnings generated from operations without the effects of financing and accounting decisions. This metric is commonly employed when comparing the profitability of different companies within the same industry, as it allows for a clearer comparison by removing variances in capital structure and tax strategies. By analyzing EBITDA, stakeholders can gain a better understanding of a company's ability to generate cash and sustain its operations over time.

ED (External Debt)

ED refers to the funds borrowed by a country from foreign sources, encompassing all debts incurred by the government, corporations, and individuals from international financial institutions or other nations. Often denominated in foreign currencies, external debt is sensitive to the borrowing country's foreign exchange reserves and fluctuations in exchange rates. High levels of external debt can increase the burden of repayment, potentially leading to economic instability, capital flight, and heightened risks of currency crises. While external debt can stimulate economic growth and facilitate capital inflows, excessive debt levels can strain repayment capacity and trigger economic crises. International credit agencies and investors assess the magnitude of a country's external debt and its ability to service this debt to determine its credit rating, which significantly influences the country's capacity to raise capital in international financial markets.

EEF (Exchange Equalization Fund)

EEF is a fund managed by the government to stabilize exchange rates. It is utilized to respond to fluctuations in specific currency exchange rates by intervening in the foreign exchange market, either by buying or selling foreign currencies to adjust the value of the domestic currency. The fund plays a crucial role in preventing economic instability resulting from rapid exchange rate changes and maintaining economic stability through the stable management of foreign exchange reserves. Typically, the Exchange Equalization Fund is established through national foreign exchange reserves, borrowings, or bond issuances. It is primarily operated by the central bank or government and serves as an essential tool for stabilizing exchange rates and preventing financial crises. By mitigating excessive fluctuations in exchange rates in the foreign exchange market, the fund promotes stability in export and import prices. In times of foreign exchange shortages or financial crises, the fund allows for the swift utilization of foreign reserves to maintain market confidence. Additionally, it helps defend or adjust the value of the domestic currency, playing a preventive role against inflation or deflation.

EITC (Earned Income Tax Credit)

EITC is a tax benefit program designed to support low-income workers. It provides tax credits or refunds to low-income individuals and families whose earned income falls below a specified threshold, aiming to reduce the burden of living expenses and encourage employment. By not only lowering taxes but also enhancing the real income of low-income households through refunds, EITC significantly contributes to economic support. The EITC primarily targets low-income workers, particularly those with children, with eligibility and benefit amounts varying based on the number of children and marital status. Individuals who meet the income criteria can receive benefits even without children, but those with children are eligible for larger credits. By offering economic incentives to low-income workers, EITC encourages employment and helps reduce dependency on welfare programs.

ELD (Equity Linked Deposit)

ELD is a financial product that links the performance of depositors' funds to the stock market. It offers the feature of capital protection while allowing the investment to be tied to stock market indices or individual stocks. This means that if the stock index rises, the depositor can earn higher returns, but even if the stock price falls, the principal is guaranteed, making it a product that seeks both stability and profitability. Typically offered by banks or financial institutions, ELDs determine interest rates based on the performance of stock indices or baskets of stocks. If the stock price rises above a specified target return, depositors can receive additional income beyond a fixed interest rate. Conversely, even if stock prices decline or show little volatility, the principal amount is protected, ensuring at least a minimal interest payout. However, there is often an upper limit on the returns, meaning that even if the stock prices rise significantly, depositors may not capture all proportional gains. Since returns are dependent on stock market performance, the success of an ELD relies heavily on the performance of the equity markets.

ELF (Equity Linked Fund)

ELF is a fund-type financial product that operates by linking investors' funds to the performance of the stock market. It invests in a variety of financial assets related to stocks, including individual stocks, stock indices, and derivatives, aiming to achieve returns that reflect stock market fluctuations. Unlike direct stock investments, ELF offers the advantage of diversification, as investors entrust their funds to professional fund managers. These managers strategically allocate capital across various stocks, indices, and derivatives, adjusting the balance between stability and profitability according to the investors' risk profiles. While similar to equity funds, ELF typically employs a broader range of financial instruments to maximize returns. Since fund managers construct and manage the investment portfolio, investors do not need to conduct their own analysis of the stock market. By investing in multiple stocks and assets, ELF allows investors to benefit from risk diversification, enhancing the overall stability of their investment.

ELS (Equity Linked Security)

ELS are derivative financial products linked to the performance of specific stocks or stock indices. Investors can earn fixed returns if the stock price rises or fluctuates within a certain range, while their principal is protected as long as the stock does not experience a sharp decline. However, there is a risk of principal loss if the stock price falls below a specified level, making ELS a product that seeks to balance risk and return compared to direct stock investments. The returns on ELS are determined based on the performance of the underlying stock index or individual stocks. Investors can receive predetermined returns as long as the stock price remains within a designated range during the investment period. ELS often includes early redemption conditions, allowing for early repayment if the stock price meets certain criteria during the investment period. This structure enables investors to pursue returns while mitigating risks compared to direct stock investments, as long as the stock market fluctuates within a specified range. However, if the stock price falls significantly, there is a possibility of losing the principal. Given the complexity of ELS and its unfamiliarity to some investors, a thorough understanding is essential before investing.

EM (Electronic Money)

EM refers to currency stored and used in digital form instead of physical cash. It is primarily stored in bank accounts, mobile wallets, or smart cards and is commonly used for online payments and e-commerce transactions. Electronic money serves as a digital alternative to cash, allowing for financial transactions without the physical movement of money through electronic transfers. Financial institutions typically issue electronic money, enabling users to convert funds from their bank accounts into digital assets or utilize mobile payment methods for real-time transactions. Electronic money can take the form of rechargeable cards or mobile applications, facilitating quick and convenient payment and remittance processes. It allows for easy handling of online payments and cross-border transactions, enabling various financial operations without the need for cash. Additionally, electronic money employs encryption technology to ensure transaction security, and usage records can be tracked, promoting transparency in transactions. However, electronic money is vulnerable to cybersecurity threats such as hacking and may be susceptible to misuse in financial crimes. Moreover, reliance on digital payment systems can lead to difficulties if technical issues arise, making it challenging to access funds or complete transactions.

EMBI (Emerging Market Bond Index)
EMBI is a key index that tracks the performance of U.S. dollar-denominated bonds issued by emerging market countries. It serves as a valuable tool for analyzing the yields, credit risks, and market volatility associated with bonds issued by governments and corporations in emerging markets, providing investors with insights into the performance of these bonds. The EMBI index, prominently offered by J.P. Morgan, is widely used as a benchmark for investments in emerging market bonds. It predominantly consists of bonds denominated in U.S. dollars and is structured based on credit ratings and maturities. EMBI reflects the credit risks and macroeconomic conditions of emerging market countries, making it useful for investors assessing the economic status and bond market risks of different nations. However, the EMBI is susceptible to the economic and political instability characteristic of emerging markets and is sensitive to fluctuations in exchange rates and liquidity shortages. As a result, the bonds included in this index are generally considered to

be high-risk assets.

EMV (Expected Monetary Value)

EMV is a statistical method used in decision-making processes to predict future monetary outcomes by calculating the weighted average of various possible results. In situations where uncertainty exists, EMV analyzes the financial impacts of different scenarios to aid in making optimal decisions. It is primarily used in project management and risk analysis, serving as a tool for quantitatively assessing potential losses or gains during project risk management. EMV is calculated by multiplying the probability of each outcome by its corresponding monetary value and summing the weighted contributions of all possible outcomes. This approach allows for a comprehensive evaluation of project risks by quantifying the financial impacts of each risk. However, a limitation of EMV is that it relies heavily on the calculated expected values. As a result, it may not accurately reflect reality in cases where the likelihood of specific outcomes is low or if the outcomes are extreme. This can lead to unrealistic expectations in risk assessments.

EOS (Economy of Scope)

EOS refers to the cost-saving benefits that arise when a company simultaneously produces multiple products or services. While similar to economies of scale—where cost per unit decreases with mass production—economies of scope focus on the efficiencies gained through the varied offerings, allowing for better resource utilization and cost reduction. When a company produces or provides multiple products or services concurrently, it can leverage shared resources such as facilities, personnel, and technology to lower overall costs. For instance, if a factory produces two different products, utilizing common resources can reduce costs compared to producing each product separately. Similarly, a software company might apply technology developed for one product to multiple products, thereby saving on additional development expenses. In marketing diversified product lines, companies can also reduce costs by sharing advertising and distribution networks. Economies of scope enhance cost efficiency in diversified businesses and create synergies, providing companies with a competitive edge. This effect is particularly pronounced in firms that produce complex products or deliver integrated services.

EPS (Earnings per Share)

EPS represents the portion of a company's profit allocated to each outstanding share of common stock, calculated by dividing the net income by the total number of outstanding shares. Here, net income is the amount remaining after deducting taxes, interest, and expenses from total revenue. EPS is a crucial metric for assessing the profitability of a company from the perspective of its shareholders, as it indicates how much profit is earned per share. Investors utilize EPS to compare the profitability of different companies or to evaluate the growth in earnings per share over time, which can inform investment decisions. A higher EPS suggests that the company is effectively generating profits, making it a key indicator of financial performance. Additionally, EPS is instrumental in calculating the price-to-earnings ratio (P/E ratio), facilitating the valuation and comparison of companies within the market.

ESI (Export Similarity Index)

ESI is a metric that measures how similarly two countries or economic regions export the same products in the global market. It assesses the degree of similarity in the export structures of the two nations and is used to analyze competitive intensity. A higher similarity suggests a greater likelihood of competition between the two countries' products. ESI is calculated by analyzing the composition of the product categories that each country exports to a specific market, determining the extent of similarity in their exported goods. The index typically ranges from 0 to 1, where a value close to 1 indicates that the export structures of the two countries are very similar, while a value near 0 suggests low similarity. Countries with high similarity in exports compete by exporting the same products, which can influence trade policies and market strategies for businesses and governments. For instance, if a company identifies a high ESI with a specific country, it may consider adopting differentiation strategies to compete effectively in that market.

ETF (Exchange Traded Fund)

ETF is an investment fund that trades on stock exchanges like a stock. It primarily tracks a specific index (e.g., S&P 500), commodity, bond, or asset class, allowing investors to achieve diversified exposure through a single investment. Listed on stock exchanges, ETFs can be bought and sold in real-time, similar to common stocks. They possess characteristics of both mutual funds and stocks; while mutual funds pool investors' capital to invest in specific assets, ETFs allow these fund shares to be traded on the market. This enables investors to diversify their portfolios with smaller amounts of capital, tracking the performance of specific indices or asset classes. ETFs facilitate quick trading, providing investors with flexibility to buy or sell when desired. Investing in a single ETF can offer exposure to multiple assets simultaneously, helping to spread risk. Additionally, they often come with lower management fees compared to traditional mutual funds, making them a cost-effective choice for long-term investment strategies. Overall, ETFs provide an accessible way for investors to diversify their portfolios while benefiting from the liquidity and trading flexibility of stocks.

EURIBOR (Euro Interbank Offered Rate)

EURIBOR is the short-term interest rate at which banks in the Eurozone lend funds to each other. It serves as a benchmark interest rate for the European interbank lending market and is applicable to transactions involving euro-denominated funds within the European Union (EU). Calculated daily based on the rates provided by major financial institutions in the Eurozone, EURIBOR is primarily used as a reference rate for various lending rates and derivative contracts. It is determined for different maturities (such as 1 week, 1 month, 3 months, 6 months, etc.), reflecting the duration for which banks are willing to lend funds. As a crucial benchmark interest rate in the euro money market, EURIBOR influences the pricing of a wide range of financial products, including residential mortgages, corporate loans, and derivatives. Additionally, it is one of the key reference rates utilized by the European Central Bank (ECB) in its monetary policy operations.

EVA (Economic Value Added)

EVA is a performance metric that assesses whether a company generates profits exceeding its capital costs. It reflects the true economic profit created by a firm, indicating how effectively it has created value above the required return expected by shareholders. EVA is calculated using the following formula:

EVA = NOPAT − (Capital Cost × Invested Capital)

Where: NOPAT (Net Operating Profit After Tax) refers to the profit a company makes from its operations after accounting for taxes. Capital Cost represents the cost incurred by the company for using capital (e.g., the return expected by shareholders). Invested Capital is the total amount invested in the company's assets.

EVA measures real profitability by considering the opportunity cost of capital, not just simple accounting profit. A positive EVA indicates that the company has created value exceeding its capital costs, while a negative EVA suggests that it has failed to cover its capital costs, resulting in economic loss.

FC (Factor Cost)

FC refers to the total cost incurred in producing goods or services, which includes the costs of the factors of production such as labor, capital, and land. It represents the direct costs associated with the production process, excluding government taxes and subsidies, making it a pure cost measurement. Factor costs are calculated based on pre-tax prices, encompassing the total costs of all production factors utilized. They do not include indirect taxes (e.g., Value Added Tax) or subsidies, thus reflecting the raw production costs from the producer's perspective. In contrast, market prices account for these indirect taxes and subsidies, representing the final price charged to consumers. Factor costs focus solely on the expenses incurred by producers for the resources used in production, providing insight into the underlying cost structure without external influences.

FC (Forward Contracts)

FC is a contract to buy or sell an asset at a predetermined price at a specific point in the future. It is traded in the over-the-counter market and is primarily used as a hedging tool to mitigate the risk of price fluctuations for various assets such as exchange rates, interest rates, and commodities. The contract is customized between the parties involved and is not standardized, thus it is conducted through direct negotiation without going through an exchange. In a forward contract, the buyer and seller agree to exchange a specific asset at an agreed-upon price on a specified future date. These contracts are mainly used for hedging purposes to reduce the risks associated with price fluctuations. For example, an exporter can reduce exchange rate risk by locking in future exchange rates through a forward contract. A forward contract is a customized agreement that allows the terms of the transaction to be set flexibly without the regulations of an exchange. This means that the terms of the contract can be tailored to specific needs. On the other hand, forward contracts may lack liquidity, and there is a risk of counterparty credit risk. In other words, there is a significant risk that the counterparty may not fulfill the contract.

FD (Final Demand)
FD refers to the total demand for final goods and services purchased by consumers, businesses, and governments in an economy, reflecting the demand for goods and services used for final consumption rather than intermediate goods. Final demand includes personal consumption, government spending, business investment, and exports, serving as a key indicator of economic growth and production activity. An increase in final demand can lead to positive effects such as expanded production and increased employment. FD plays an important role in the calculation of Gross Domestic Product (GDP) and is used to understand and predict economic conditions. Policymakers analyze changes in final demand to adjust economic policies aimed at promoting consumption and investment and stimulating the economy, with the goal of achieving long-term economic growth.

FD (Financial Derivatives)
FD refers to financial products whose prices fluctuate based on the value of underlying assets (e.g., stocks, bonds, commodities, currencies, etc.). They have no intrinsic value by themselves; instead,

their value is determined by changes in the prices of the underlying assets. They are used for hedging (risk management) and speculation (investment aimed at profit) and help investors and businesses manage risk and explore opportunities for profit generation. Derivatives are utilized to reduce the risk of price volatility through hedging or to maximize returns through investment. For example, an exporting company that faces risks due to currency fluctuations can use futures contracts to mitigate those risks. Additionally, investors can leverage derivatives to expect high returns with relatively low capital. However, derivatives carry a high degree of speculation, which can expose investors to significant risks. In particular, incorrect predictions or volatility can lead to losses, necessitating specialized knowledge and careful management.

FE (Fountain Effect)

FE is a concept in economic theory that describes the phenomenon where the government's large-scale fiscal expenditure gradually spreads throughout the entire economy, leading to economic activation and income growth. It contrasts with the trickle-down effect, illustrating a structure where policy effects initiated at the lower levels of the economy spread upward. This primarily involves implementing economic policies centered around low-income individuals, suggesting that their consumption and expenditure create positive ripple effects throughout the economy. The fractional effect argues that when the government supports low-income groups or implements policies for income redistribution and welfare expansion from the bottom up, the consumption of these groups increases, resulting in overall income growth and economic expansion. In other words, it is a policy approach that aims to induce economic recovery by reducing income inequality and promoting consumption. The fractional effect emphasizes the importance of empowering lower-income individuals as a catalyst for broader economic growth and stability.

FOP (Free of Payment)

FOP refers to a method in financial or securities transactions where the transfer of assets or securities occurs without the payment being settled. It is typically used in situations where the settlement and asset transfer are separated, contrasting with the concept of Delivery versus Payment (DVP). In FOP transactions, assets are delivered, but payment does not occur simultaneously. FOP is commonly used in international securities transactions or commercial deals, where the ownership of the asset is transferred, but the payment for it is processed separately at a later date. This method is applied when only part of the transaction is processed first due to differences in calculation methods or transaction structures. In securities trading, investors often receive the transfer of assets or securities first, while the payment is handled separately, primarily in global financial markets. FOP structures can also be used in credit transactions where payment is made after a certain period. Since the transfer of assets is separate from payment, there may be credit risks or payment default risks associated with the transaction counterparties. Therefore, trust between counterparties becomes an essential factor to mitigate these risks.

FRN (Floating Rate Note)

FRN refers to a bond with an interest rate that is adjusted periodically. Instead of a fixed interest rate, the rate fluctuates based on market interest rates, typically determined by adding a certain spread to benchmark rates like LIBOR or EURIBOR. This type of bond is attractive to investors looking to manage interest rate risk, as the interest payments vary with changes in market rates. The interest rate on an FRN is adjusted regularly, usually every three or six months. Since the interest rate is linked to market rates, if rates rise, the interest rate on the FRN will also increase, allowing investors to expect higher returns. Conversely, if rates fall, the interest rate will decrease as well. FRNs provide the advantage of potentially higher interest income during periods of rising rates while ensuring regular interest payments, making them adaptable in terms of yield.

FRS (Fractional Reserve System)

FRS refers to a banking operation system where banks hold only a fraction of the funds deposited by customers as cash reserves and use the rest for loans or investments. In other words, banks can operate under the assumption that not all deposited funds need to be withdrawn immediately, allowing them to keep a certain percentage of deposits in cash while utilizing the remainder. In the fractional reserve system, a reserve ratio is established to regulate the proportion of deposits that banks must hold. For example, if the reserve ratio is 10%, the bank must keep 100,000 out of 1,000,000 won as reserves, allowing the remaining 900,000 won to be loaned or invested for profit. The fractional reserve system promotes economic growth and enables credit creation by allowing banks to provide loans using deposited funds. As long as customers do not withdraw all their deposits at once, banks can maximize profits through lending and investing while maintaining reserves. However, if a situation arises where customers attempt to withdraw large amounts of deposits (a bank run), and the bank does not have sufficient reserves, it may face a liquidity crisis. If the reserve ratio is too low, it can lead to instability in the entire financial system.

FT (Futures Transaction)

FT is a contract to buy or sell an asset (e.g., commodities, currencies, indices, etc.) at a predetermined price at a specific point in the future. It involves an agreement to deliver the asset and pay the price on a set date, and it is traded as standardized contracts on exchanges. Futures are primarily used for hedging (risk management) and speculation, playing a crucial role in reducing risks associated with price fluctuations or pursuing profits. In futures trading, the buyer and seller of the asset enter into a contract at an agreed price for a future date. Contracts are standardized according to exchange regulations and are mainly traded for assets such as commodities (crude oil, gold), currencies, and stock indices. The clearinghouse guarantees contract fulfillment, reducing credit risk. Futures trading provides investors with leverage, allowing them to trade with relatively small capital. However, the use of leverage also increases the potential for losses, and there may be an obligation to either deliver the asset or pay cash on the expiration date. Companies can use futures trading to hedge against risks arising from fluctuations in commodity prices or exchange rates. Investors may utilize futures trading to seek profits from price changes. For example, if they anticipate a rise in gold prices, they can buy gold futures contracts to pursue profits.

FV (Face Value)

FV refers to the nominal value of a financial instrument such as bonds, stocks, or banknotes. It is the amount indicated on the financial instrument; for example, in the case of bonds, it refers to the principal amount paid to investors at maturity. For stocks, it represents the official nominal price of the shares issued by the company, but it may differ from the actual market price. In bonds, FV indicates the principal amount that investors will receive at maturity. For instance, a bond with a face value of 5,000 won will pay 5,000 won to the investor at maturity. Interest payments on bonds are typically calculated based on this FV. In the case of stocks, the face value refers to the official price set by the company when issuing the shares. However, stocks are usually traded at prices higher than the face value in the market, and the market price is determined by supply and demand.

FWM (Fixed Weighted Method)

FWM is a measurement method used to evaluate price fluctuations or quantity changes in economic indicators or statistical analyses. It assesses the changing prices or production volumes over time using the weights from a specific base year. In other words, it tracks economic changes such as inflation rates or economic growth rates through fixed weights. In FWM, weights are established based on the prices or quantities from the base year, and these weights are applied consistently across all subsequent evaluation periods. This allows for a consistent comparison of variations across different years. For example, when calculating the Consumer Price Index (CPI), fixed weights can be assigned to each item based on a stable consumption pattern. Since the weights are fixed, FWM enables consistent comparison of data from various time points. Because the weights are constant, calculations are relatively simple, making it easy to observe trends in data changes. However, FWM may not adequately reflect changes in consumer patterns or economic structures over time. For instance, it is challenging to account for economic fluctuations resulting from technological advancements or changes in consumer preferences.

FX (Foreign Exchange)

FX refers to the exchange of one currency for another. It is the largest financial market in the world, where various transactions occur for the immediate exchange of currencies or for exchange at a specific future date. FX trading is primarily conducted for purposes such as international trade, investment, travel, and international finance. The FX market, also known as the foreign exchange market, allows for the free trading of currencies from different countries.

GAAP (Generally Accepted Accounting Principles)

GAAP refers to the accounting principles and standards that companies in the United States must adhere to when preparing financial reports. It provides rules and guidelines to ensure that a company's financial condition and performance are reported accurately and consistently. This allows stakeholders such as investors, regulatory agencies, and creditors to trust financial statements and facilitates comparisons between companies. It includes criteria for when revenue should be recognized and principles for accurately recording expenses based on when they are incurred. GAAP requires that financial reports accurately reflect a company's actual financial condition. It ensures consistency in accounting, making it easier to compare financial reports across different companies. Additionally, it allows investors and shareholders to make informed decisions based on reliable information. The U.S. Securities and Exchange Commission (SEC) requires publicly traded companies to report their finances in accordance with GAAP.

GDI (Gross Domestic Investment Ratio)

GDI refers to the ratio of a country's domestic investment to its Gross Domestic Product (GDP). It is an important indicator that shows the extent to which a country invests capital for economic growth, primarily including fixed investments in facilities, construction investments, and inventory increases. GDI is useful for assessing economic development and growth potential. It is calculated by including investments in fixed assets (e.g., factories, machinery, buildings) and changes in inventories. Generally, a higher domestic investment rate indicates a greater likelihood of robust economic growth, as capital accumulation enhances future productivity. GDI represents the level of investment activity in a country and serves as a critical economic indicator for predicting future growth potential.

GDP (Gross Domestic Product)

GDP is an economic indicator that measures the total value of goods and services produced within a country or region over a specific period (usually a year or a quarter). It is one of the most important measures of the overall scale of economic activity and is primarily used to assess a country's economic growth and for international economic comparisons. GDP is divided into nominal GDP and real GDP, with real GDP being adjusted for inflation. It serves as a key indicator for measuring economic growth rates, with higher GDP indicating a more active national economy. GDP is a crucial benchmark for governments and economic experts in formulating economic policies. It plays an important role in comparing national economic power internationally and analyzing economic shocks or business cycles. However, while GDP can provide a rough estimate of the standard of living, it has limitations as it does not fully reflect aspects such as income distribution, wealth inequality, or quality of life.

GDR (Global Depositary Receipts)

GDR is a financial instrument issued by a company to allow foreign investors to trade its domestic shares. It provides a means for a company to trade its domestic shares in overseas markets using foreign currencies such as dollars or euros, enabling it to raise funds in international capital markets. It is commonly used by multinational corporations or companies planning to expand overseas. GDRs are issued by depositary banks, which hold the company's domestic shares and then issue receipts based on those shares to global investors. Investors can buy and sell GDRs in their local currency, which provides the same rights as the actual shares. This allows companies to offer trading opportunities to global investors, while investors can easily trade various stocks across different countries.

GDS (General Depreciation System)

GDS is one of the asset depreciation methods used in U.S. tax law, where a fixed amount is depreciated each year based on the asset's useful life. It follows the MACRS (Modified Accelerated Cost Recovery System) to calculate the depreciation expense for assets. This reflects the decrease in the asset's value over time as it is used, allowing the business to benefit from tax deductions. GDS applies standardized depreciation lives (e.g., 3 years, 5 years, 7 years) for specific types of assets, spreading the cost over that period. The fixed depreciation period varies based on the asset type, enabling tax deduction of costs over the asset's useful life. In addition to GDS, there is an alternative depreciation method known as ADS (Alternative Depreciation System), which uses longer depreciation periods for assets and is applied in cases of specific regulations or long-term assets.

GFCF (Gross Fixed Capital Formation)

GFCF refers to the total amount of fixed capital formation, measuring the net increase in fixed assets (such as buildings, machinery, equipment, and roads) investment within an economy. It serves as a significant indicator of economic growth, indicating how much a country or economy has invested in physical capital to enhance future productivity. GFCF plays a crucial role in increasing a country's productive capacity by including investments in long-term assets like machinery, infrastructure, and construction, reflecting the level of capital investment that promotes long-term economic growth. A high growth rate in GFCF is interpreted as a signal that the country is investing more capital for economic growth. Therefore, GFCF is considered an essential indicator for analyzing a country's economic policies and investment direction.

GL (General Ledger)

GL is an accounting book that records and manages all financial transactions of a business, including all accounts and transaction details necessary for financial statement preparation. It categorizes transaction details by accounts such as assets, liabilities, equity, revenue, and expenses, allowing for a systematic understanding of the company's financial status. This facilitates the accurate preparation of the income statement and balance sheet at the end of the accounting period. The GL plays a critical role in maintaining the transparency of financial reporting, minimizing accounting errors, and accurately assessing the company's financial condition and performance. Each transaction is generally recorded with the date, amount, and relevant account codes, enabling systematic management of financial records in preparation for audits.

GL (Gross Loss)

GL refers to the total gross loss incurred by a company over a specific period, occurring when the result of total revenue minus the cost of goods sold is negative. This indicates that the cost of goods sold exceeded the total revenue generated from selling products or services. Gross loss reflects issues in the cost structure or inefficiencies in production and operations, serving as an indicator of deteriorating business performance. When the cost of goods sold is higher than total revenue, a negative value arises, signifying that the company sold products but incurred a loss due to higher production costs. Addressing gross loss is crucial for businesses to enhance profitability and improve overall operational efficiency.

GMA (Geometric Moving Average)

GMA is a moving average technique used in financial data or stock price analysis, which calculates the average of data over a specified period using geometric means to reflect volatility. It is commonly used to more accurately understand changes over time in stock prices, exchange rates, or commodity prices. Unlike the traditional Simple Moving Average (SMA), GMA has the advantage of better reflecting multiplicative changes in data such as returns. The data values for a specific period are calculated using the geometric mean, which is useful for analyzing ratio data like returns and is derived by taking the root of the product of the values. GMA is effective in assessing the long-term volatility of stocks or financial instruments and is particularly useful for handling ratio-based data. It is less sensitive to sharp fluctuations in data, providing a smoothed trend. Compared to SMA, GMA better reflects percentage changes like returns or growth rates, allowing for a more accurate representation of actual changes in the data.

GNI (Gross National Income)

GNI is an indicator that reflects a country's Gross Domestic Product (GDP) plus income earned from abroad (such as income from assets owned by foreigners) and income paid to foreigners. It represents the total income earned by the citizens of a country, both domestically and internationally, and is an important measure for assessing the economic standard of living and the total economic activities of its citizens. GNI provides a more accurate representation of personal income or the real income levels of a nation's citizens.

GP (General Provisions)

GP refers to the general reserves established by financial institutions to prepare for potential losses. Unlike provisions set for specific risks, this reserve is created to manage the overall risk of loss for the company, serving as a sort of fund to cover unexpected losses in the future. It is primarily established by banks or financial institutions to manage loan-related risks. GP acts as a contingency fund for possible losses that may arise from specific assets, considering the general risk of loss rather than being limited to a particular transaction or asset. As such, it is recorded as a provision in accounting and plays a crucial role in evaluating a company's financial soundness in financial statements. GP helps financial institutions prepare for unforeseen losses that may occur in uncertain economic conditions, thereby maintaining financial stability and strengthening risk management. Additionally, GP is set aside as a contingency asset according to accounting principles, even if losses have not yet occurred, making it essential for capital management and liquidity management within financial institutions.

GP (Gross Profit)

GP represents the amount remaining after subtracting the Cost of Goods Sold (COGS) from the total revenue generated by a company through the sale of its products or services. It serves as a key indicator for assessing the profitability derived from a company's core operating activities, excluding other costs such as operating expenses, taxes, and interest expenses. GP indicates how efficiently a company manages its costs and generates revenue through its core operations. A higher GP suggests that the company is effectively controlling the costs associated with producing its products or services, resulting in greater profits.

GVA (Gross Value Added)

GVA refers to the net value added created by a country or business through production activities, calculated by subtracting intermediate consumption (the costs of raw materials or services used) from the total production value. GVA is a critical component of Gross Domestic Product (GDP), enabling the evaluation of contributions from various sectors within the economy and facilitating comparisons between industries. It represents the actual economic value generated during the production process and is used to assess productivity and efficiency in both businesses and national economies. GVA is utilized in the calculation of GDP, reflecting economic activities before adjusting for taxes and subsidies. Therefore, GVA serves as an important benchmark for forecasting future developments and determining strategic directions in economic policy formulation and business strategy development.

GVC (Global Value Chain)

GVC refers to the global supply chain in which companies from various countries collaborate during the production and distribution of goods and services. It describes the flow of added value that occurs across a globally dispersed process involving production, assembly, and distribution, from raw material supply to final consumers. Companies seek to maximize cost efficiency by leveraging differences in costs, technology, and labor across countries. The economic growth of a country is not limited to its own production capacity but is closely linked to the production networks and economic activities of other countries. GVC plays a crucial role in global trade and enhances interdependence among nations. It is widely used by multinational corporations to optimize production and distribution efficiently across the globe. Companies utilize the cost structures and technological capabilities of different regions to enhance their global competitiveness. Governments can also use GVC to formulate economic development policies and strengthen their role in international trade.

HDI (Household Disposable Income)

HDI represents the net income that a household can actually use after deducting taxes, social insurance contributions, and other expenses. It is an important economic indicator that reflects the household's consumption capacity, used for various spending such as housing costs, food expenses, and education fees. HDI plays a crucial role in assessing the actual living standards and income distribution of households. It is calculated by subtracting taxes and social security contributions from total income. This figure indicates the money that households can save or spend, and it is used to measure the economic stability and purchasing power of households. Household disposable income is one of the key indicators for evaluating a country's living standards and economic well-being, as higher income allows households to engage in more consumption and savings. It serves as an important reference for formulating economic policies, directly reflecting the impacts of tax policies and welfare systems.

HE (Hidden Economy)

HE is a term that encompasses economic activities that are omitted from official government statistics or tax reporting. It consists of informal transactions that involve tax evasion, illegal activities, or non-compliance with legal reporting obligations, and since these activities are not officially recorded, they make it difficult to accurately assess the size of the economy. The hidden economy can lead to a reduction in government revenues and economic distortions. Tax evasion weakens the government's ability to provide public services, while illegal activities can cause social instability and economic imbalance. Additionally, the difficulty in accurately determining the size of the economy can create confusion in policy decision-making. Addressing the hidden economy is essential for fostering transparency and enhancing the effectiveness of economic policies.

HHI (Herfindahl-Hirschman Index)

HHI is used to evaluate the level of competition in a specific market. It is calculated based on the market shares of firms within that market and plays an important role in assessing monopolies or market competition structures. The higher the concentration of firms, the greater the value of the HHI, which is used to evaluate the risk of monopoly. If HHI ≤ 1,500, the market is considered competitive, with low concerns about monopolies. If 1,500 < HHI ≤ 2,500, it indicates a moderately concentrated market, where some risk of monopoly may exist. If HHI > 2,500, the market is highly concentrated, suggesting a greater risk of monopolies. HHI is primarily used by antitrust regulatory authorities to analyze market competitiveness during mergers and acquisitions (M&A) and serves as an important reference for establishing market competition policies. If market concentration sharply increases due to mergers or acquisitions between firms, regulatory authorities may restrict such transactions.

HSS (Hybrid Settlement System)

HSS is a system that processes fund settlements by combining the features of Real-Time Gross Settlement (RTGS) and a net settlement system. It utilizes the speed of RTGS and the liquidity efficiency of net settlement to reduce settlement delays and optimize fund usage. This helps financial institutions manage settlement risks while effectively maintaining liquidity. HSS supports efficient fund settlements in international payments and fund transfers between financial institutions, enhancing the stability and efficiency of the financial system. Central banks of various countries can mitigate risks in the financial system and ensure settlement stability through HSS, facilitating smooth global financial transactions. HSS plays a crucial role in promoting confidence and reliability in the financial infrastructure.

IB (Investment Bank)

IB is a financial institution that provides services such as financial advisory and capital raising to corporations, governments, and institutional investors. It specializes in large-scale financial transactions, including corporate finance, mergers and acquisitions (M&A), securities issuance, and trading of stocks and bonds, playing a different role than that of commercial banks. Investment banks efficiently facilitate large financial transactions and act as important intermediaries in the financial markets. This enables corporations and governments to secure funding for large projects or quickly respond to market changes.

IC (Intermediate Consumption)

IC refers to the consumption of inputs used by a country or economic entity to produce goods or services. It includes resources that are consumed in the production process rather than final consumption, encompassing materials, fuel, electricity, and services used by producers to complete products or services. It serves as an important economic indicator for measuring the production costs of enterprises. Intermediate consumption is calculated based on the value of all intermediate goods and services used by producers to create final consumer goods. This does not refer to the completed products but rather consists of resources before value is added. IC plays a crucial role in understanding the scale of resources consumed in the total production process of a country. A higher level of intermediate consumption indicates that more resources were used in the production process, providing useful data for analyzing the economic structure and efficiency.

ICO (Initial Coin Offering)

ICO is a method by which block chain or cryptocurrency projects raise funds by issuing and selling digital tokens. It is similar to a traditional IPO (Initial Public Offering), but it differs in that it involves the issuance of cryptocurrencies instead of shares. ICOs are widely used as a way to secure funding during the early stages of a project, with investors purchasing tokens in anticipation of the project's future value. During an ICO, investors buy the project's cryptocurrency tokens, which can later be traded or used depending on the project's success. The project team collects funds during the ICO period to continue development, and the tokens may be used as utility within the future platform or listed on exchanges. While ICOs can offer the potential for high returns, they also carry significant risks due to a lack of regulation and the possibility of project failure leading to investment losses. Some ICOs have been revealed to be fraudulent projects, so investors should carefully review the project's whitepaper and the credibility of the team.

IF (Indirect Financing)

IF refers to a method where financial institutions act as intermediaries to supply funds, meaning that businesses or individuals obtain financing through banks, insurance companies, and other financial institutions. Fund seekers can secure the necessary funds by either taking out loans directly from financial institutions or purchasing securities issued by these institutions. Financial institutions collect deposits from depositors and provide them in the form of loans, generating operating income through interest revenue. Indirect finance simplifies the funding process and enhances stability, as the financial institutions manage the associated risks. This method is primarily used when small businesses or individuals find it challenging to raise funds directly from capital markets. Indirect finance plays a crucial role in the economy, especially as financial institutions conduct credit assessments and risk management to ensure the safety of fund supply.

IFRS (International Financing Reporting Standards)

IFRS is the international standard for financial reporting established by the International Accounting Standards Board (IASB). It was created to maintain consistency in the preparation of financial statements globally and to ensure that stakeholders can clearly understand financial information. IFRS provides uniform accounting rules worldwide, reducing confusion caused by differences in accounting standards between countries and enhancing the transparency and reliability of international capital markets. In the past, each country used its own accounting standards, making it difficult to compare the financial positions of multinational companies. However, IFRS allows for the preparation of financial statements using the same standards across various countries, simplifying the process for investors and financial institutions to compare and analyze companies across borders. This plays a crucial role in enhancing corporate credibility and improving the efficiency of capital raising in a globalized economic environment. IFRS standardizes the treatment of assets, liabilities, revenues, and expenses, enabling consistent financial reporting. As a result, companies adopting IFRS can transparently report their financial status according to internationally recognized standards, providing essential information to investors, regulatory authorities, and other stakeholders.

ILG (Income-Led Growth)

ILG is an economic strategy that focuses on increasing the income of households and workers to promote consumption, making it a key driver of economic growth. By raising wages, creating jobs, and expanding social welfare, it aims to enhance consumer capacity and stimulate the domestic market, which in turn encourages increased revenue for businesses and job creation. This shifts the foundation of economic growth toward a domestic focus, promoting stable and sustainable growth. Income-led growth emphasizes reducing the economic burden on low-income and middle-class groups and alleviating income inequality. It aims to strengthen social stability and enable long-term economic growth while addressing issues of economic inequality. ILG has established itself as a strategy that supports organic economic growth by enhancing the purchasing power of citizens through welfare and wage policies.

IOT (Input-Output Tables)

IOT is a tool used to analyze the economic interactions between various industrial sectors within a country or regional economy. It systematically illustrates how goods and services produced in the economy during a specific period are used by different industrial sectors and ultimately delivered to consumers. This allows for the assessment of how much each industry relies on others and provides insights into the interlinkage structure among industries in the overall economy. The IOT is based on a model developed by economist and statistician Wassily Leontief, quantifying the inputs (goods purchased by one industry from another) and outputs (goods produced by an industry supplied to other industries or final consumers) in tabular form. For example, the automotive industry purchases raw materials such as steel, electronic components, and plastics to produce vehicles, which are then supplied to other industries or consumers. The input-output table records these processes in detail. The IOT plays a crucial role in the analysis of various economic policies.

IRR (Internal Rate of Return)

IRR is a financial metric used to evaluate the profitability of investment projects, defined as the discount rate that makes the net present value (NPV) of future cash flows from an investment equal to zero. It represents the expected return on invested capital and serves as a critical criterion for determining whether an investment project is profitable. IRR is widely used in capital budgeting, investment decisions, and comparative assessments of various investment projects. If a company or investor calculates the IRR for a specific project and finds that the return exceeds the minimum required return (typically the discount rate or cost of capital), the project is considered economically viable. Conversely, if the IRR is below the required return, the project is deemed unworthy of investment. For example, if a project's IRR is 10%, this means that a 10% annual return can be expected on the investment. If the IRR exceeds the company's cost of capital (e.g., 8%), the investor may see it as more beneficial to proceed with the project. A key advantage of IRR is that it intuitively reflects investment profitability, making it easy for investors to understand. However, IRR may not be a suitable evaluation tool for all projects. In cases where cash flow structures are complex or involve multiple outflows relative to the initial investment, IRR can yield multiple values or become distorted, necessitating caution.

IRS (Interest Rate Swaps)

IRS is a financial contract in which two parties exchange interest payments on their debts with different interest rate terms. It is primarily conducted by exchanging fixed and floating interest rates, allowing each party to secure a favorable interest rate environment. For example, a company that has borrowed at a fixed rate might want to benefit from floating rates, so it can swap its fixed rate for a floating rate with a counterparty who has a floating rate loan, thereby reducing interest rate risk. Interest rate swaps play a crucial role in helping corporations and financial institutions manage interest rate fluctuations and optimize funding costs. They are particularly useful in maintaining a stable financial structure in environments with significant interest rate volatility and are widely utilized as derivative instruments for capital management and risk hedging. IRS has become an essential risk management tool in the financial markets of various countries.

IT (Impossible Trinity, Impossible Trilemma)

IT refers to the economic theory that a country cannot simultaneously achieve three goals: fixed exchange rates, independent monetary policy, and free capital movement. In an increasingly open global economy, this concept represents a significant monetary policy dilemma faced by nations, indicating that "only two out of the three can be chosen." Countries must choose two of these three objectives and forfeit the third. For example, to maintain fixed exchange rates and free capital movement, a country must give up independent monetary policy, suggesting that its monetary policy may be constrained by external factors.

JB (Junk Bond)

JB are high-risk, high-yield bonds issued by companies with low credit ratings and a relatively high likelihood of default. They offer attractive interest rates to lure investors, but they are characterized by significant repayment risks due to the unstable financial condition of the issuing companies. Most junk bonds receive low ratings from credit agencies for this reason. Junk bonds provide high returns for investors willing to take on substantial risks, while also serving as a financing method for companies. Typically, startups or financially unstable companies issue junk bonds to raise funds, and investors seek returns through the yields offered by these bonds. However, during economic fluctuations or worsening financial conditions of the issuing companies, the risk of loss is high, necessitating a cautious investment approach.

KIKO (Knock-In Knock-Out)

KIKO are derivative products whose activation or extinction depends on exchange rate fluctuations, primarily used for currency hedging purposes. This product activates the option when the exchange rate reaches a specific level (Knock-In price) and extinguishes it when it reaches another specific level (Knock-Out price). Companies use KIKO options to reduce risks associated with exchange rate fluctuations and to expect exchange gains when the rates move within a certain range. KIKO is sensitive to exchange rate volatility and can pose significant risks; if the exchange rate moves unexpectedly, it can lead to substantial losses. In particular, if the exchange rate reaches the knock-out level and the option is extinguished, the hedging effect is lost, increasing the risk of additional losses. KIKO is commonly used by small and medium-sized enterprises to manage currency risks, but due to its high risk, careful analysis and planning are required.

KYC (Know Your Customer)

KYC refers to the procedures that financial institutions use to verify the identity of their customers, understand their financial activities, and assess potential risks. It is primarily applied to comply with regulations such as Anti-Money Laundering (AML) and Combating the Financing of Terrorism (CFT). KYC includes the process of confirming whether customers are trustworthy individuals or entities when they utilize financial services. Typically, financial institutions require official documents such as identification (e.g., passport, driver's license) and ask customers about the purpose of their transactions or the source of their funds. Through this process, financial institutions can confirm customers' identities and determine whether their transaction activities are associated with illegal actions. Additionally, regular monitoring is conducted to manage and prevent any suspicious transaction activities. KYC is a necessary procedure implemented by various financial service providers, including not only financial institutions but also cryptocurrency exchanges, fintech companies, and insurance firms. As international anti-money laundering regulations strengthen, the KYC process has become increasingly important.

LBO (Leveraged Buy Out)

LBO is a method of acquiring a company using external funds such as loans or bond issuances to purchase the target company. Acquirers obtain loans or issue bonds using the assets of the acquired company as collateral, allowing them to make large acquisitions with a relatively small amount of capital. This method is particularly common among private equity firms and investment companies. LBOs can expect high returns, but they also increase financial risk due to the added debt burden after the acquisition. If the acquired company generates sufficient cash flow, the acquirer can maximize profits through debt repayment; however, if cash flow is lower than expected, management difficulties may arise. LBOs are used as part of high-return investment strategies but carry significant risks.

LCR (Liquidity Coverage Ratio)

LCR is a regulatory metric used to assess a financial institution's ability to respond to short-term liquidity crises. It was introduced as part of the Basel III regulatory framework to manage liquidity risk in banks following the financial crisis. LCR indicates whether a financial institution has sufficient High-Quality Liquid Assets (HQLA) to operate stably even in extreme stress situations for 30 days. The LCR value is calculated as the percentage of high-quality liquid assets divided by the expected net cash outflows over a 30-day period. If the LCR is 100% or higher, it means that the financial institution can sufficiently meet its expected liquidity needs without having to sell assets or convert them to cash for 30 days. Conversely, if it is below 100%, there is a higher likelihood that the institution may face a liquidity crisis. The LCR regulation requires banks to hold sufficient liquid assets, leading to a more conservative strategy in short-term cash management. This enhances the stability of the financial system, although profitability may be somewhat limited.

LDR (Law of Diminishing Returns)

LDR refers to the principle in economics that describes the phenomenon where, after a certain point, adding more of a production factor results in progressively smaller increases in output. This concept is frequently mentioned in production processes such as agriculture and manufacturing and is important for analyzing the efficiency of resource allocation. It explains the outcomes when one production factor (e.g., land, machinery, capital) is held constant while additional units of another production factor (e.g., labor, materials) are added. Initially, adding more factors can lead to significant increases in output, but after a certain point, the additional contributions of these factors begin to diminish. For example, increasing the number of workers on a fixed plot of farmland may initially boost yields, but beyond a certain number of workers, the rate of productivity gains may decline, and eventually, it could even lead to reduced output. The law of diminishing returns plays a crucial role in various economic decision-making processes, such as resource allocation, labor management, and capital investment.

LE (Leverage Effect)

LE refers to the impact of utilizing debt or borrowed capital to undertake investments that are larger in scale than equity capital alone, thereby increasing returns. It is commonly employed by companies to utilize capital more efficiently when purchasing assets or executing projects, and it can contribute to a higher return on equity (ROE). The leverage effect involves not only using equity but also leveraging additional borrowed capital to make larger investments. If the return on the investment exceeds the interest costs of the borrowed capital, investors can achieve greater profits through leverage. For example, when investing in real estate, instead of investing solely with equity capital, taking out a loan can significantly increase returns if asset prices rise.

LGD (Loss Given Default)

LGD is a metric that indicates the actual loss percentage incurred by a financial institution or investor when a borrower defaults. It refers to the proportion of the asset that cannot be recovered when the borrower fails to repay their debt. This metric plays a crucial role in credit risk analysis, helping financial institutions measure and manage credit losses on loans. LGD is essential for evaluating the risk associated with a loan portfolio and formulating policies to minimize losses. In particular, loans with a higher likelihood of default may reflect a higher LGD, prompting the institution to set aside additional capital. This assists banks in ensuring they have adequate capital to cover potential losses from non-performing loans, thereby contributing to the stability of the financial system. LGD is typically calculated by estimating the percentage of recoverable assets in the event of default. For example, if a loan amount is 10 billion won and the amount recoverable upon default is 3 billion won, the LGD is calculated as 70%, indicating that 70% of the total loan amount is an irrecoverable loss. The formula for LGD is as follows:

LGD = (Loss Amount) / (Total Loan Amount) = 1 − (Recovery Rate)

Here, the Recovery Rate represents the proportion of the asset that the creditor can recover in the event of default; the higher the recovery rate, the lower the LGD.

LT (Liquidity Trap)

LT is a phenomenon where monetary policy fails to stimulate the economy in situations where interest rates are very low or close to zero. In such cases, despite interest rate cuts or additional liquidity supply, economic agents tend to hold cash or avoid consumption and investment. When a liquidity trap occurs, providing more liquidity to stimulate the economy may not be effective, leading to an increased risk of deflation. A liquidity trap highlights the limitations of traditional interest rate policies of central banks, necessitating additional fiscal policies or unconventional monetary policies. For example, the government may increase public spending, or the central bank may use unconventional methods such as Quantitative Easing (QE) to stimulate demand and boost the economy. LT typically occurs during economic downturns and has been notably observed in countries like Japan. In such situations, a more comprehensive approach is needed to restore consumer and business confidence and achieve sustainable economic growth. To overcome the liquidity trap, policymakers should consider a combination of monetary and fiscal policies.

LTV (Loan to Value Ratio)

LTV is an indicator that shows the ratio of the loan amount to the value of the collateral asset when financial institutions provide loans. It is primarily used in mortgage loans and serves as a benchmark for evaluating how much loan a borrower can receive compared to the value of the asset they offer as collateral. For example, if the LTV is 70%, it means that with a collateral value of 1 billion won, a maximum loan of 700 million won can be obtained. A high LTV ratio poses a risk for financial institutions because borrowers can receive loans exceeding the collateral value, which reduces the amount that can be recovered in the event of a decline in real estate prices or an economic downturn. Therefore, financial institutions aim to manage the LTV ratio appropriately to mitigate risks and maintain a stable loan portfolio.

MACRS (Modified Accelerated Cost Recovery System)

MACRS is a method of asset depreciation according to U.S. federal tax law that allows for the early recognition of depreciation expenses, enabling larger costs to be deducted during the initial periods after asset acquisition. Introduced by the Tax Reform Act of 1986, it is designed to allow businesses to quickly recover costs associated with newly acquired assets and to benefit from tax savings early on. This method provides a favorable structure for businesses to rapidly depreciate assets such as equipment or machinery, helping them to recoup initial investment costs and reduce taxes. The primary goal of MACRS is to facilitate the early recovery of investment costs in company assets, thereby encouraging new capital expenditures or asset acquisitions. This allows businesses to improve cash flow and reinvest capital more quickly. Additionally, early depreciation helps reduce tax burdens, enabling businesses to secure funding for expansion.

MBS (Mortgage Backed Securities)

MBS is a type of financial instrument issued based on the cash flows generated from residential mortgage loans. After financial institutions provide mortgage loans, they bundle these loan receivables into MBS, allowing investors to receive principal and interest payments from the underlying mortgage loans. MBS is primarily issued by housing finance agencies or private financial institutions, playing a crucial role in facilitating funding for the housing market and providing investors with various investment opportunities. It helps channel funds into the housing market, enabling financial institutions to offer more loans. Additionally, investors gain the opportunity to invest indirectly in the housing market through MBS. Financial institutions create a loan pool by aggregating individual mortgage loans, which serves as the underlying asset for MBS issuance. The securitization process involves this loan pool, enabling the distribution of cash flows (principal and interest) from the mortgage loans to investors. Investors receive distributions of the principal and interest generated from the mortgage loans in exchange for purchasing MBS. They can expect stable cash flows and interest income based on the credit rating of the MBS. However, MBS acted as a significant risk during the financial crisis of 2008 due to falling real estate prices and widespread defaults. Since then, regulations related to MBS issuance have tightened, and investors have become more vigilant in managing risks.

MMF (Money Market Fund)

MMF is a type of open-end fund that invests in short-term financial instruments to seek stable returns. It primarily diversifies investments in low-risk financial products with short maturities, such as short-term bonds, government bonds, and commercial paper (CP), providing investors with relatively low risk and liquidity. MMFs offer advantages similar to bank deposits in terms of yield and liquidity, but they can provide higher returns compared to bank deposits. Due to their high liquidity and stable yields, MMFs are suitable for investors managing short-term funds or emergency cash. Additionally, when market interest rates rise, the yields on MMFs tend to increase quickly, allowing for favorable returns depending on economic conditions. Consequently, MMFs serve as an effective tool for investors seeking to balance risk and return while maintaining access to their capital.

MOS (Margin of Safety)

MOS refers to the buffer set to protect against losses in investment or management decision-making. It aims to minimize the risk of price decline and enhance safety by securing a stock price that is lower than the intrinsic value of the investment. This concept is widely known as a core principle among value investors such as Benjamin Graham and Warren Buffett, helping investors adopt a more cautious and defensive approach against stock price fluctuations. MOS is a useful metric not only for analyzing corporate value but also for making investment decisions in uncertain economic situations. By carefully assessing intrinsic value to secure a MOS, investors can reduce potential losses and achieve stable long-term investment returns. In particular, MOS plays a more critical role in investment decisions during periods of increased market volatility. Through MOS, investors can avoid unexpected losses and secure reliable profits. MOS is calculated as the difference between a stock's intrinsic value and its current market price. For example, if the intrinsic value of a particular stock is 10,000 won and it is trading at 7,000 won in the market, the MOS would be 30%. Generally, the higher the MOS, the greater the safety perceived by the investor.

MPB (Monetary Policy Board)

MPB is the key body within the central bank responsible for determining financial and monetary policy, primarily adjusting the benchmark interest rate and establishing various monetary policies necessary for economic stabilization. In South Korea, the Bank of Korea's Monetary Policy Board performs this role, aiming for price stability, employment promotion, and economic growth. It ensures overall economic stability and growth through various measures, including adjusting interest rates, regulating liquidity supply, and implementing exchange rate stabilization policies, according to the economic situation. The Bank of Korea's Monetary Policy Board consists of the governor and vice governors, along with other members, who discuss and decide on policies independently. The MPB holds regular meetings to discuss economic conditions and can convene emergency meetings as needed.

MTM (Mark to Market)

MTM is an accounting method that evaluates assets or liabilities based on their current market prices. This approach reflects the value of held assets or liabilities in real-time according to market value, primarily used to accurately represent fluctuations in the value of financial instruments or investment assets. The advantage of MTM is that it provides a more realistic view of a company's financial condition, allowing investors and stakeholders to clearly understand the current value of assets. It is mainly applied to the assets held by financial institutions or investment companies, and is particularly used for assets with significant market price fluctuations, such as stocks, bonds, and derivatives. For example, in the case of derivative contracts or tradable securities, MTM assesses profitability and risk by reflecting market price changes in real-time. While MTM accurately represents asset values and provides a precise financial condition, it also carries the risk of significantly impacting a company's financial statements during periods of high market price volatility. For instance, sudden changes in the financial markets can lead to a sharp decline in asset values, resulting in unexpected losses that negatively affect a company's creditworthiness and financial stability. During the 2008 global financial crisis, MTM immediately reflected declines in the asset values of certain financial institutions, causing shocks to the financial markets.

MVA (Market Value Added)

MVA is an indicator that represents the amount by which a company's market value exceeds the capital provided by its investors, serving as a key performance metric for measuring how efficiently a company creates shareholder value. It is calculated by deducting the invested capital from the company's market value, and a higher MVA indicates that the company has effectively utilized its capital to generate additional market value. MVA is useful for maximizing shareholder value and evaluating a company's long-term growth potential. It is widely used as a performance metric for companies aiming to maximize shareholder value, as a high MVA signifies that the company is using its capital effectively and is being valued highly in the market, reflecting investor confidence and positive expectations. Conversely, a negative MVA indicates that the company is creating less value than the invested capital, suggesting low management efficiency or negative market perception.

NCD (Negotiable Certificate of Deposit)

NCD is a financial product that issues deposited funds in the form of a certificate, which can be transferred to other investors before maturity. It is issued by banks and differs from regular deposits in that it can be freely traded on exchanges or in over-the-counter markets. It is considered a highly liquid asset because it can easily be converted into cash before maturity. NCDs are used as a short-term investment tool, allowing financial institutions to raise short-term funds while investors can expect higher returns compared to regular deposits. They are particularly advantageous for corporations and financial institutions seeking flexibility in cash management and are commonly used as a means for managing short-term funds. NCDs are classified as relatively safe investments, with interest rates determined by the creditworthiness of the issuing bank.

NDC (Net Debit Caps)

NDC is a system in payment systems that limits the net debit (liabilities) cap that each financial institution can incur over a specified period to manage risk. This helps prevent excessive liabilities within the payment system and maintains overall system stability. The net debit cap is set by the central bank or the operator of the payment system and is assigned differently based on the creditworthiness and transaction volume of each institution. NDC plays a crucial role in mitigating payment risks among financial institutions within the payment system and preventing instability in the financial system due to payment defaults. It enhances the reliability and stability of payment systems and supports financial institutions in conducting transactions securely.

NDF (Non-Deliverable Forward)

NDF is a forward exchange contract that settles the cash difference between the agreed-upon exchange rate at the time of the contract and the spot exchange rate at maturity, without the actual delivery of the underlying asset. It is primarily used for trading currencies from countries with strict foreign exchange regulations, and it allows for different currencies to be set for the contract and settlement. NDF helps businesses and investors manage the risks associated with currency fluctuations. It is widely used as a hedging instrument for regulated currencies in the international forex market and provides convenience by settling only the difference without actual currency exchange. For example, NDF can be used for currencies like the Korean won (KRW) to mitigate currency risk and manage volatility. Due to its cash settlement feature, NDF serves as an effective tool for adjusting risk. This characteristic has made NDF a useful method for companies to minimize losses due to currency fluctuations and has contributed to global investors managing forex risk and implementing more flexible investment strategies.

NDI (National Disposable Income)

NDI is an indicator that represents the total income that households and the government can freely consume and save after deducting taxes and other deductions from the total income earned by a country in a year. NDI is calculated by adding the income received from abroad to the Gross National Income (GNI) and subtracting the income sent abroad. It plays a significant role in understanding the consumption power of households and the economic conditions of the country, and it is used as a measure to evaluate economic growth and living standards. Through this, the government can establish policies to stimulate consumption or encourage savings, and devise measures to enhance the actual living standards of the citizens.

NEER (Nominal Effective Exchange Rate)

NEER is an indicator that reflects the strength or weakness of a country's currency against multiple major trading partner currencies. It is calculated by averaging the exchange rates of the country's currency against the currencies of its trading partners, allowing for a comprehensive evaluation of the nominal value of the currency across the entire economy rather than just in relation to a single country. NEER is generally more helpful than simple exchange rate indicators for understanding the foreign exchange market conditions of a country. The calculation of NEER primarily uses the ratios of exports and imports to major trading partners as weights, which assess whether the domestic currency is strong or weak against the currencies of trading partners. For example, if a country mainly exports goods to the United States and China, the fluctuations in the exchange rates of the US dollar and Chinese yuan will significantly impact the NEER calculation. If the domestic currency appreciates on average against the currencies of major trading partners, the NEER will rise, indicating that domestic products may become relatively more expensive and export competitiveness may weaken. Conversely, a lower NEER suggests that the prices of domestic products become more competitive, potentially boosting exports. NEER plays a crucial role in measuring the impact of exchange rate changes on trade and in formulating economic policies. For instance, central banks may reference the NEER indicator to establish exchange rate policies aimed at preventing the currency value from becoming excessively high or low. Additionally, since NEER is a nominal exchange rate that does not account for price levels, it is more appropriate to evaluate actual purchasing power, considering inflation, through the Real Effective Exchange Rate (REER).

NGDP (Nominal Gross Domestic Product)

NGDP is an economic indicator that reflects the total production of a country over a specific period at current market prices, without adjusting for price fluctuations. It is calculated using the price levels of the year in question, directly influenced by inflation or deflation. While NGDP is useful for understanding the size of the economy and growth trends, it has limitations in assessing real economic growth since it does not take price changes into account. To address this, Real Gross Domestic Product (RGDP) is used, and NGDP, along with RGDP, plays a significant role in economic analysis. It is essential to interpret NGDP with the consideration that growth may be overestimated due to price increases.

NGT (New Growth Theory)

NGT is an economic theory that views technological innovation, knowledge accumulation, and human capital as the primary drivers of economic growth. Unlike traditional growth theories, it argues that economic growth does not rely on external factors (like technological advancement), but rather that innovation and knowledge production within the economy enable sustained growth. Therefore, it emphasizes the significant role of innovation activities by businesses and individuals in driving economic growth. This theory suggests that government investments in education, support for research and development, and incentives for corporate innovation can promote sustainable growth. As human capital and knowledge accumulate in the economy, productivity improves, and long-term growth potential expands. NGT is widely used as a theoretical basis for growth policies in modern economies, especially in technology-driven industries.

NI (Net Income)

NI is a financial metric that represents the actual profit remaining after deducting all expenses, taxes, and interest from the revenue earned by a company over a specific period. It reflects the net amount of profit that the company ultimately generates and is often referred to as the "Bottom Line," as it appears at the bottom of the income statement. Net income serves as a key indicator for assessing a company's operational performance, profitability, efficiency, and financial health. It includes not only the operating income generated from business activities but also the profits and costs associated with investment or financing activities, as well as all expenses like taxes. For example, if a company earns revenue from selling products during a given period, net income is calculated by subtracting all expenditures, including production costs, operating expenses, employee salaries, interest expenses, and taxes, from that revenue. The resulting amount is the net income, which represents the actual profit available for distribution as dividends to shareholders or reinvestment in the business. Net income is an important decision-making tool for management, investors, and shareholders. A consistent increase in net income signals effective cost management and revenue generation, interpreted as a positive indicator. Conversely, a decline in net income or a loss may indicate the need for cost structure improvements or strategies to enhance profitability. Additionally, net income forms the basis for calculating Earnings Per Share (EPS), which serves as an important reference for investors assessing a company's profitability and growth potential.

NI (Nominal Income)

NI refers to the total income of individuals, households, or businesses measured at current market prices without considering inflation. Unlike real income, it does not reflect the effects of price changes, representing the absolute amount of income earned at a given time. It expresses the amount in monetary units, and in situations of inflation or deflation, it may not accurately reflect the real purchasing power of that income. While nominal income serves as a fundamental indicator for measuring economic conditions and assessing individuals' income levels, caution is necessary when interpreting it due to its lack of adjustment for price level changes. For instance, if nominal income increases over a period but inflation rises beyond that increase, the actual purchasing power could decrease. Conversely, in a stable price environment, an increase in nominal income may indicate an improvement in real living standards. Therefore, it is important to evaluate changes in nominal income alongside inflation-adjusted real income. Nominal income plays a crucial role in economic analysis and policy-making. For example, the government can analyze the average nominal income of citizens to determine the absolute size of purchasing power and use that information to formulate tax or welfare policies. Additionally, individuals or households can plan their budgets and expenditures based on nominal income, while financial institutions may evaluate loan limits based on nominal income as well.

NIM (Net Interest Margin)

NIM is a ratio that represents the profitability of a financial institution, calculated by dividing the difference between the interest income earned from loans and investments and the interest expenses paid on deposits by the total operating assets. A higher NIM indicates greater ability of the financial institution to generate profits. This figure reflects the earnings arising from the spread between lending rates and deposit rates and is primarily used to assess the profitability of banks. NIM is an important indicator for analyzing the operational performance of financial institutions and predicting changes in profits due to interest rate fluctuations. For example, if lending rates increase while deposit rates remain stable, NIM will rise, leading to improved profitability for the financial institution. Conversely, a decrease in NIM could indicate a reduction in profits, negatively affecting profitability.

NL (Net Loss)

NL refers to the loss incurred when a company's total revenue is less than its total costs and expenses, resulting in a negative remaining amount. This situation occurs when the total costs incurred from operating, investing, and financing activities exceed the total revenue generated over a specific period. A net loss indicates a deterioration in the company's financial condition, which can arise from factors such as declining asset values, increasing liabilities, or poor operational performance. A net loss negatively impacts a company's profitability and, if persistent, may lead to a reduction in capital or a management crisis. To address this, companies typically strive to improve their net loss by implementing strategies such as cost reduction, revenue enhancement, and operational efficiency. Ultimately, managing and mitigating net losses is crucial for ensuring long-term sustainability and financial health.

NM (Natural Monopoly)

NM refers to a market situation in which strong economies of scale make it more efficient for a single company to supply the entire market. This phenomenon typically occurs in public service sectors or foundational industries such as electricity, gas, water, and railroads, where high initial investment costs and substantial fixed operating expenses can lead to inefficiencies if multiple companies compete and duplicate investments. In a natural monopoly scenario, even if one firm dominates the market, it can provide services to consumers at a lower cost. Natural monopolies emerge in industries where economies of scale allow for cost-saving effects, meaning that as production increases, the cost per unit continues to decline. For example, in the electricity sector, the initial costs of generating power and establishing the power grid are very high, but this allows the supply of electricity to many consumers. If multiple companies attempted to build and operate their own power grids, the resulting duplicate investments would sharply increase costs, leading to higher rates for consumers. Therefore, having one company monopolize the entire market reduces social costs and maximizes economic efficiency. However, natural monopolies can also lead to issues where the dominant firm may raise prices arbitrarily or lower the quality of services due to its monopolistic position. For this reason, industries characterized by natural monopolies are typically subject to government regulation and oversight. Governments impose regulations such as price controls and quality management to protect consumers and maintain the quality of public services, and they may choose to operate these industries directly as public enterprises to ensure citizens have access to essential services.

NNI (Net National Income)

NNI refers to the actual income of a country's citizens during a specific period after subtracting depreciation from the total income generated. It is a crucial indicator for measuring the net income of the entire national economy, representing the portion of income earned by citizens through productive activities that is actually available for use. NNI is calculated by subtracting the depreciation of capital assets from Gross National Income (GNI), helping to evaluate economic performance more realistically. Depreciation refers to the reduction in value of fixed assets such as equipment, machinery, and buildings over time. Since NNI indicates the income that citizens can actually utilize, it serves as an important metric for assessing the living standards and economic welfare of the population. For instance, even if a country's GNI increases, significant depreciation of capital assets could reduce the actual income available for citizens. NNI reflects this by considering the decline in asset value, providing a more accurate representation of a country's real economic achievements. It plays a vital role in evaluating economic growth rates and the living standards of citizens, as well as in understanding consumer capacity and overall economic stability. NNI is also important in economic policy formulation and analysis; for example, the government can use the NNI metric to predict citizens' disposable income and consumption possibilities, which can inform tax policies, social security systems, and economic growth strategies. Additionally, NNI is a significant indicator for international comparisons, serving as a more useful metric than GNI when comparing living standards and economic welfare between countries. Since NNI reflects the income that citizens can actually spend, it becomes an essential criterion for realistically understanding economic performance.

NOC (No Occupancy Cost)

NOC refers to a situation where tangible assets remain vacant, generating no income while incurring ongoing maintenance costs.

This occurs when landlords are unable to find tenants, leading to a lack of rental income despite the continuous occurrence of fixed costs such as management fees, taxes, and maintenance expenses. If the vacancy persists for an extended period, it can place a significant financial burden on the landlord. This situation is particularly problematic in the commercial real estate and rental housing markets, where the longer the vacancy lasts, the greater the cost burden becomes, necessitating effective tenant acquisition strategies from the landlord's perspective. When no occupancy costs arise, landlords often consider various strategies to address the vacancy issue. For example, they may need to offer promotions such as rent reductions, initial rent waivers, or flexible lease terms to attract tenants. While these incentives can result in short-term reductions in revenue for landlords, they may prove beneficial in the long run by alleviating the no occupancy costs associated with maintaining a vacant property. Additionally, some landlords may adjust rental conditions flexibly to reduce the tenant's burden and quickly resolve vacancies. NOC can serve as an important indicator of supply and demand imbalances in the real estate market, with an increase in vacancies often signaling a downturn in the market. This phenomenon is especially prevalent during periods of economic instability and consumer contraction, leading to an increase in no occupancy costs in commercial and residential rental properties. Therefore, real estate owners must closely analyze market conditions to mitigate vacancy risks and adjust their tenant acquisition strategies to minimize the burden of no occupancy costs.

NOE (Non-Observed Economy)

NOE refers to economic activities that are not captured in official government statistics or reports, often referred to as the informal economy or implicit economy. It encompasses officially unrecorded economic activities, including tax evasion, illegal activities, informal employment, household production, and self-sufficiency forms of economic activity. This concept is important for evaluating the actual size of the economy, addressing economic activities that the government fails to include in official GDP figures. NOE manifests in various forms, primarily categorized into informal economy, illegal economy, and unreported economic activities. For instance, the informal economy includes jobs or transactions conducted informally to evade taxes or regulations, while the illegal economy encompasses unlawful economic activities like drug trafficking and smuggling. Additionally, unreported economic activities refer to legal undertakings that are not included in official statistics, such as self-production or informal trading. Thus, NOE contributes to understanding the hidden aspects of the economy that are not reflected in statistics. It affects economic policy and revenue forecasting, prompting governments to accurately assess NOE to address potential revenue shortfalls and mitigate the ripple effects of the informal economy across the economy. Particularly, when NOE constitutes a significant portion of the economy, it can diminish economic transparency and undermine the fairness of tax and regulatory systems. Consequently, many countries are developing new statistical methods to capture NOE and strengthening institutional efforts to reduce unreported economic activities.

NOI (Net Operating Income)

NOI is an indicator that reflects the pure operating profitability of a real estate asset, defined as the amount remaining after subtracting operating expenses from total operating income. Here, operating income includes rental income and other real estate-related revenues, while operating expenses encompass costs such as insurance premiums, taxes, and maintenance fees, excluding non-operating expenses like interest costs and depreciation. NOI is crucial for assessing how much income a real estate asset generates, making it widely used in real estate investment decision-making. It also plays an important role in real estate valuation, particularly when calculating the asset's capitalization rate (Cap Rate). A higher NOI indicates stronger asset profitability, serving as a positive signal for investors. Conversely, a low NOI may suggest high operating costs or low revenues, indicating the need for improvements.

NP (Notional Principal)

NP refers to a hypothetical principal amount used in derivative transactions, serving as a benchmark for calculating the actual cash flows of the contracts. Although it is not exchanged directly in the transaction, it acts as the basis for interest payments or profit calculations between the parties involved. For example, in transactions such as interest rate swaps or currency swaps, the NP is the reference amount for calculating interest payments. This amount is a notional principal specified in the contract and is not actually exchanged, meaning there is no direct cash movement resulting from the transaction. The nominal principal plays a critical role in deriving income and costs associated with the interest rates or fluctuations in rates related to the derivatives. For instance, when Company A and Company B agree to exchange fixed and floating interest rates in an interest rate swap, each party exchanges interest based on the nominal principal according to the agreed-upon interest rates. Here, the NP is only used to calculate the interest flows between the two companies and is not transferred in reality. This allows the parties to manage interest rate risk or secure the desired interest income.

NPV (Net Present Value)

NPV refers to the amount obtained by subtracting the initial investment cost from the present value of expected future cash flows. It is a widely used metric for evaluating the profitability of investment projects, allowing investors to reassess the actual value of an investment by converting future cash flows to today's value. A positive NPV indicates that the investment is likely to generate returns above expectations, while a negative NPV suggests that the investment will yield lower returns than anticipated. NPV applies a discount rate when converting future cash flows to their present value. The discount rate is a critical factor in determining the present value of future cash flows and is typically set based on the investor's target return or market interest rates. In NPV calculations, an increase in the discount rate results in a lower present value of future cash flows, while a decrease leads to a higher present value. For example, the NPV of a specific investment project might be positive at a 5% discount rate but could turn negative if the rate is increased to 10%. Thus, the choice of an appropriate discount rate is crucial, as it significantly affects the NPV outcome.

NSFR (Net Stable Funding Ratio)

NSFR is a metric used to assess whether banks have sufficient stable funding to mitigate liquidity risk over the long term. Introduced under the Basel III regulations, it encourages financial institutions to reduce reliance on short-term funding fluctuations and secure stable funding over an extended period. The purpose of NSFR is to manage the maturity mismatch between a bank's assets and liabilities, ensuring a stable liquidity supply even in times of economic stress. NSFR is calculated by dividing the bank's Available Stable Funding (ASF) by the Required Stable Funding (RSF), with a ratio of 100% or more indicating the ability to fund operations stably. ASF includes capital, deposits, and long-term borrowings that are relatively stable and have longer maturities, while RSF refers to assets that require stable funding due to their shorter maturities or lower liquidity. For instance, if a bank relies solely on short-term borrowing while providing long-term loans, the NSFR would decrease, increasing liquidity risk. Maintaining an NSFR above 100% allows banks to secure funding reliably over the long term, enabling them to respond better to external shocks such as economic downturns or financial crises. This contributes not only to the stability of the banks but also to the overall stability of the financial system, as regulatory authorities aim to reduce systemic risks by ensuring compliance with NSFR regulations.

OB (Offshore Banking)

OB refers to financial activities where individuals open bank accounts and manage assets in countries outside of their residence. This practice typically offers advantages such as tax benefits, asset protection, and regulatory leniency, and is commonly conducted in countries with lower tax rates or less stringent financial regulations. Individuals and businesses utilize offshore bank accounts to diversify their assets internationally and reduce taxes. Offshore banking serves as a means for asset protection and tax optimization, helping to enhance asset security and distribute financial risks. However, in some countries, this practice may be viewed as a potential avenue for tax evasion or money laundering, leading to increased regulatory scrutiny. While offshore banking provides diversity in asset management within the international financial market, compliance with the legal regulations of various countries is essential.

OCC (Occupancy)

OCC is a metric that indicates the proportion of total space actually being used in specific facilities such as real estate, hotels, and hospitals. It plays a crucial role in assessing the utilization of commercial properties or diagnosing the operational status of hotels and hospitals.

For example, in real estate, the OCC is calculated as the ratio of the area occupied by tenants to the total rentable space, while in hotels, it refers to the percentage of rooms that have been booked and are actually being used by guests. Occupancy rate is an important indicator for evaluating the profitability and operational efficiency of a facility. A high occupancy rate signifies that the facility is being effectively utilized, which may indicate high profitability. Conversely, a low occupancy rate suggests significant vacancies, indicating inefficient operation of the asset, thus requiring improvement. For instance, if a hotel has a high OCC during a particular season, it indicates strong booking demand, presenting an opportunity to increase rates, while hospitals can manage bed occupancy to optimize the quality of healthcare services. OCC serves as an important reference indicator for investment decisions and management strategy formulation. Real estate investors and management teams can assess the operational status of their assets through changes in occupancy rates, adjusting marketing strategies or rental policies accordingly. Additionally, a high occupancy rate for a specific building or facility can serve as a basis for considering future investments or expansion plans.

OI (Operating Income)

OI refers to the amount obtained by deducting operating expenses from the revenue generated through a company's core business activities, serving as an important financial indicator of how effectively a company generates profit from its primary operations. It is used to evaluate the profitability derived from basic business activities, such as producing goods and providing services. Operating income is calculated from the income statement by subtracting operating costs, such as Cost of Goods Sold (COGS) and Selling, General and Administrative Expenses (SG&A), from total sales revenue, excluding non-operating revenues and expenses, interest, and taxes. It plays a crucial role in assessing a company's operational efficiency and intrinsic competitiveness. A high operating income indicates that a company effectively manages its costs or experiences steady revenue growth. Conversely, a decline in operating income or a loss may suggest issues with operational efficiency. For instance, if a company consistently generates revenue but incurs excessive costs or selling and administrative expenses, its operating income may decrease, negatively impacting its financial condition. OI is utilized by investors and management to assess the company's fundamental profitability and make strategic decisions. The higher and more stable the operating income, the more likely investors are to positively evaluate the company's growth potential, allowing management to develop various strategies, such as cost reduction and sales strategy adjustments, based on this information.

OPEX (Operating Expenditures)

OPEX refers to the costs a company incurs to maintain its daily operations, including expenses necessary for producing goods and providing services. Items categorized under OPEX include employee salaries, raw material costs, energy expenses, advertising costs, rent, and maintenance expenses, which directly impact the company's operational performance. OPEX is recorded as operating expenses on the income statement, showing the total costs incurred to generate revenue. It serves as an important indicator for evaluating a company's profitability and operational efficiency. When a company effectively manages OPEX, the ratio of costs to revenue decreases, contributing to an increase in operating income (OI) and net income (NI). For instance, if a company can reduce costs while maintaining the same level of revenue, the resulting difference enhances profitability. Conversely, an increase in OPEX can lead to a decline in operating income, negatively affecting the company's profitability. Therefore, businesses prioritize cost management and continuously strive to optimize OPEX. OPEX is utilized by management as a benchmark to enhance efficiency and target cost reductions. Executives analyze OPEX items to identify areas for unnecessary spending reductions or methods to improve operational efficiency. For example, strategies may involve using resources more efficiently or adopting new technologies to reduce maintenance costs, necessitating OPEX optimization.

ORA (Official Reserve Assets)

ORA refers to the foreign exchange reserves, gold, Special Drawing Rights (SDR), and reserve assets held by a country's central bank for international transactions. These official reserve assets are used for stabilizing exchange rates, intervening in foreign exchange markets, and facilitating international payments, playing a crucial role in defending the national currency and maintaining economic stability during foreign exchange crises or external shocks. ORA serves as a key indicator of a country's creditworthiness, helping to assess its ability to repay external debt and respond to external economic instability. A country with sufficient official reserve assets is more likely to maintain stability during a foreign exchange crisis, which acts as a positive signal to international investors and contributes to enhancing economic credibility.

OS (Operating Surplus)

OS refers to the remaining profit after deducting operating costs and fixed capital consumption from the total production of a business or the economy as a whole. It signifies the pure profit generated primarily through the company's operating activities, after accounting for wages, interest, and taxes. This metric plays a crucial role in evaluating the operational efficiency of a business and measuring capital profitability. Operating surplus is calculated by excluding labor costs and production taxes from Gross Value Added (GVA), making it useful for assessing a company's profitability and making investment decisions. In the broader economic context, it represents the surplus of the pure production sector excluding households and the government, serving as an indicator of the productivity and growth of the national economy.

OTC (Over-The-Counter)

OTC refers to the method of trading securities or financial products directly between individual financial institutions rather than through a designated exchange. In the OTC market, stocks, bonds, and derivatives are primarily traded, allowing for flexible trading conditions and customized contracts. While OTC trading is not subject to exchange regulations, enabling a wider range of products and structures to be traded, it also comes with the downside of lower liquidity and transparency, potentially increasing risk. OTC is commonly utilized by institutional investors to trade complex financial products tailored to their specific needs, allowing companies to implement unique risk management and financing strategies. The OTC market offers various financial products that cater to specific investor demands, providing the flexibility to transact outside of established exchange regulations.

PAC (Planning Advisory Committee)

PAC is a committee that provides advice to achieve strategic goals related to economic and financial management. This committee brings together experts and stakeholders to offer various recommendations to ensure that economic plans and financial policies pursued in the public and private sectors are effectively and sustainably realized. PAC plays a crucial advisory role, particularly in areas related to economic development, financial management, and investment planning, with experts from each field participating to comprehensively review the impact of policies on local communities and economic environments. The committee gathers opinions from the community and industry during the economic policy decision-making process and suggests policy directions. For example, when large-scale infrastructure investments or local economic revitalization programs are initiated, PAC analyzes the impact of these projects on the local economy and assesses financial risks and opportunities to help ensure that policies can achieve realistic objectives.

PB (Protection Buyer)

PB refers to the party that purchases protection to mitigate credit risk in credit derivative transactions. In the event of a credit event (such as default or a downgrade in credit rating), the protection buyer acquires credit protection from a protection seller to receive compensation for losses. These credit derivatives are primarily traded in the form of Credit Default Swaps (CDS), where the protection buyer pays a premium similar to an insurance premium, and the protection seller assumes the liability for compensation. The protection buyer serves to reduce the credit risk associated with their held assets or loans. For example, if a bank holds bonds from a specific company and is concerned about the potential deterioration of that company's credit status, it can become a protection buyer through a CDS contract. By paying the premium, the protection buyer can receive loss compensation in the event of a credit event, enabling effective risk management. Thus, the protection buyer plays a crucial role in enhancing the stability of an asset portfolio and mitigating potential financial shocks. This mechanism is vital for maintaining confidence in financial markets and managing systemic risk.

PBR (Price on Book-value Ratio)

PBR is a ratio that compares a company's market capitalization (stock price) to its book value (asset value), used to assess whether the company's stock is overvalued or undervalued relative to its actual asset value. It is calculated by dividing the stock price by the book value per share, serving as a useful reference for investors to determine if the stock price is appropriate based on the company's asset value. This ratio indicates how closely the stock price is linked to the company's net assets and is commonly used in the stock market. A PBR greater than 1 indicates that the market capitalization exceeds the book value, suggesting that the stock is valued higher than its asset value. Conversely, a PBR less than 1 indicates that the stock is undervalued compared to its book value. For example, a PBR of 1.5 means the stock is valued 50% higher than its asset value, while a PBR of 0.8 means it is undervalued by 20%. Investors use this ratio to evaluate investment opportunities based on asset value and to identify potentially undervalued stocks in the market. Generally, a lower PBR suggests that the stock price is undervalued compared to asset value, which could present a potential investment opportunity; however, this does not necessarily guarantee a good investment opportunity.

PD (Probability of Default)

PD is an indicator that reflects the likelihood of a borrower defaulting on their obligations within a specified period, serving as a crucial component in credit risk assessment. It is calculated by considering factors such as the borrower's financial condition, credit history, and the economic environment, and is primarily used by financial institutions to measure and manage risk during loan evaluations and asset portfolio management. A higher PD indicates a greater likelihood that the borrower will fail to repay their debt. PD is significantly utilized in credit risk models, assisting financial institutions in ensuring adequate capital against potential losses. By combining PD with loss given default (LGD), institutions can estimate expected loss (EL), which forms the basis for determining loan interest rates and developing risk management strategies. Additionally, PD is widely used in corporate credit assessments and financial product investment analysis.

PDI (Personal Disposable Income)

PDI refers to the income that individuals can freely use for consumption or savings after deducting taxes and mandatory contributions such as social security. It is the remaining amount from an individual's total income after subtracting taxes and compulsory deductions, representing the income that can be spent or saved at one's discretion. PDI is an important indicator for assessing an individual's standard of living and spending capacity, and it is used to understand consumption patterns and savings rates depending on the economic situation. Changes in PDI significantly impact consumer spending and economic activity. When disposable income increases, individuals have more capacity for consumption, positively affecting the economy; conversely, a decrease in disposable income can lead to reduced spending and potential economic slowdown. For example, if the government lowers taxes, PDI may rise, stimulating consumer spending, which contributes to domestic demand and economic growth. On the other hand, if taxes increase or prices rise, PDI may decrease, leading to reduced consumption.

PED (Price Elasticity of Demand)

PED measures how much the quantity demanded of a good respond to changes in its price. It assesses consumers' price sensitivity by calculating the percentage change in quantity demanded relative to the percentage change in price. A PED value greater than 1 indicates high sensitivity to price changes, categorizing demand as elastic, while a value less than 1 signifies inelastic demand. PED plays a crucial role in understanding consumer behavior and informing pricing strategies for businesses. For example, essential goods (such as food) typically exhibit low price elasticity, as demand remains relatively stable despite price increases, resulting in a low PED. Conversely, luxury items (like designer clothing) tend to have high price elasticity; a price rise can lead to a significant drop in demand, thus reflecting a high PED. Therefore, understanding price elasticity is vital for businesses when developing pricing policies.

PER (Price Earnings Ratio)

PER is a ratio that measures a company's current share price relative to its earnings per share (EPS), helping to assess whether the stock is overvalued or undervalued in relation to its profitability. A high PER suggests that the market has a positive outlook on the company's future growth potential, while a low PER may indicate that the stock is undervalued. This metric plays a crucial role in enabling investors to evaluate stock value and make informed investment decisions. For example, comparing PERs within the same industry can help identify relatively undervalued companies. However, since PER can be influenced by various factors such as growth potential and economic fluctuations, it is essential to analyze it alongside other financial metrics.

PG (Payment Gateway)

PG is a system that securely mediates the transmission of payment information between consumers and merchants during online transactions. It helps ensure that the card information or bank account details entered by the consumer are encrypted before being transmitted to the merchant, thus facilitating secure processing. PG supports various payment methods, including credit cards, debit cards, and e-wallets, simplifying the payment process for online transactions while enhancing security for both consumers and merchants. The payment gateway guarantees the safety of transactions through the encryption of payment information and the approval process. When a consumer enters payment information, the PG encrypts this data and transmits it to the payment network or bank for authorization, then sends the approval back to the merchant. In this process, the PG strengthens security to prevent sensitive payment information from being exposed and supports various digital payment methods, including card payments, mobile payments, and QR code payments.

PI (Payment Instruments)
PI refers to the various methods used by individuals to pay for goods and services. Common payment instruments include cash, credit cards, debit cards, e-wallets, mobile payments, and bank transfers. These payment methods offer convenience and security, and with technological advancements, new forms of digital payment instruments are rapidly emerging. Payment instruments facilitate transactions between consumers and businesses, playing a crucial role in promoting economic activity. Notably, the development of digital payment methods, such as electronic payments, has made transactions faster and more convenient, leading to an increase in contactless transactions and global commerce. PI contributes to the flow of funds in the economy and enhances financial accessibility.

PI (Property Income)
PI refers to the income generated from assets owned by individuals, primarily including interest, dividends, and rental income. Unlike labor income, property income arises from the ownership of assets,

such as real estate, stocks, bonds, and deposits. It plays a crucial role in enhancing the economic stability of individuals and households by providing an important means to generate additional revenue through asset utilization. The main components of property income include interest income, dividend income, and rental income. Interest income is derived from financial assets such as deposits or bonds, while dividend income refers to the payments received by shareholders from stock investments. Rental income is generated from rental fees associated with real estate assets, which individuals or businesses earn by leasing their properties.

PL (Profit and Loss Statement)

PL is a financial statement that records a company's revenues and expenses over a specific period to calculate the net profit or loss. It determines operating income by subtracting the cost of goods sold (COGS) and operating expenses (SG&A) from sales revenue, and further calculates the final net profit by deducting interest expenses, taxes, and other costs. This statement allows for the assessment of a company's operational performance and profitability. The profit and loss statement is a crucial resource for investors, management, and financial institutions to analyze the company's financial health and profitability. It helps in identifying profitability trends and provides insights into cost efficiency and revenue structure.

PLG (Profit-Led Growth)

PLG is an economic theory that posits that an increase in profits is a primary driver of economic growth. In PLG, when corporate profits rise, it stimulates investment and increases employment, ultimately promoting economic growth. This type of growth is primarily achieved through expanded corporate investment, productivity improvements, and technological innovations, with profit increases leading to heightened overall demand and supply in the economy. The profit-led growth model emphasizes the impact of corporate profits on economic growth and utilizes strategies such as tax cuts, deregulation, and infrastructure investment to achieve growth objectives. It contrasts with consumption-led growth and is often adopted in industrial economies where capital investment and productivity enhancement play crucial roles.

PM (Primary Market)

PM refers to the market where new securities are initially issued and sold to investors. In this stage, corporations, governments, and other entities issue stocks or bonds for the first time to raise funds, allowing individual and institutional investors to purchase these securities directly. The primary market plays a crucial role in bringing new capital into the economy, which helps companies expand their operations or secure working capital. Notable examples include IPOs (Initial Public Offerings) and bond issuances. Through an IPO, a company issues shares to the public for the first time, enabling it to raise capital from a wide range of investors. Additionally, governments or public institutions issue bonds in the primary market to fund social infrastructure projects or welfare programs. As this market is where securities are initially created, the issue price is determined by the supply and demand dynamics between the issuing entity and the investors, impacting the price at which the securities will trade in the secondary market. After securities are first issued in the primary market, they are traded in the secondary market, where transactions occur between investors.

PO (Put Option)

PO is a financial product that grants the holder the right to sell a specific asset at a predetermined price on a future date. An investor holding a put option can profit when the price of the underlying asset declines, and it can be applied to various assets, including stocks, bonds, and commodities. If the market price of the underlying asset falls below the strike price (exercise price), the investor can exercise the put option to realize a profit. Put options serve as a risk management tool against price declines and are frequently used to hedge against the downside risk of a portfolio. By utilizing put options, investors can minimize losses when asset values decrease and protect their holdings in uncertain market conditions.

PPI (Producer Price Index)

PPI is an economic indicator that measures the price changes of goods and services sold by producers, evaluating inflationary trends. It primarily reflects the price changes of raw materials and intermediate goods, helping to assess price dynamics before they reach consumers. PPI tracks price fluctuations across various industries, including agriculture, energy, and manufacturing, making it a crucial indicator for predicting inflationary pressures. An increase in producer prices can influence consumer prices (CPI), acting as a factor that contributes to overall inflation. Central banks and policymakers use PPI to adjust economic policies, including interest rate strategies and economic stabilization measures.

PPP (Purchasing Power Parity)

PPP is a concept of exchange rates that adjusts for the value of money and price levels between countries, ensuring that identical goods can be purchased at the same cost in different nations. This theory compares the real purchasing power of currencies based on each country's price levels and assumes that when exchange rates are adjusted, the prices of goods remain consistent across borders. Essentially, PPP suggests that currencies achieve equilibrium when they have the same purchasing power. It serves as an important indicator in international economic analysis, mainly for predicting long-term exchange rate levels and understanding differences in living costs between countries. An example of PPP is the "Big Mac Index," which compares the prices of a Big Mac burger worldwide to assess whether currencies are overvalued or undervalued. While PPP implies that identical goods should cost the same across countries, actual exchange rates can vary due to factors like supply and demand, interest rates, and trade flows. Therefore, PPP is useful for identifying discrepancies between reality and theory and for predicting long-term economic trends.

PR (Principal Risk)

PR refers to the possibility of losing the invested principal due to the counterparty's default in a financial transaction. This risk arises when a transaction is not fulfilled or when the agreed funds are not returned to the investor, indicating a potential loss of the principal amount. It can occur in various financial contexts, including foreign exchange trading, bond investments, and derivatives trading. Principal risk is a critical aspect of risk management for both financial institutions and investors, especially in large or complex transactions, where the potential loss of principal can have significant financial repercussions. This risk is closely related to the credit risk of the counterparty. For example, if Bank A conducts a foreign exchange transaction with Bank B and Bank B fails to fulfill the contract, Bank A may lose its principal due to the counterparty's default. To mitigate this risk, financial institutions employ strategies such as credit assessments, collateral arrangements, and adjustments to contractual terms. Additionally, in transactions with high principal risk, techniques such as central clearing or the use of credit derivatives may be implemented to enhance risk mitigation.

PS (Protection Seller)

PS refers to a party in a credit derivative transaction who assumes credit risk and is responsible for compensating the protection buyer in the event of a default by a specific debtor. In exchange for receiving a premium from the protection buyer, the protection seller agrees to provide debt repayment or compensation if a credit event (such as default or downgrade) occurs. A prominent example is in Credit Default Swaps (CDS), where the protection seller takes on the credit risk of the debtor, allowing them to generate income. The protection seller earns a certain return by bearing the credit risk and plays a crucial role in risk diversification. In the credit market, the credit protection offered by the protection seller allows the protection buyer to reduce credit risk, thereby ensuring the stability of their portfolio. Simultaneously, the protection seller manages risk by analyzing the creditworthiness of the counterparty and the terms of the contract, contributing to the overall stability of the financial system through credit risk diversification.

PT (Program Trading)

PT refers to a trading method that utilizes computer algorithms and automated systems to quickly and efficiently trade large volumes of stocks or financial products. Transactions are executed automatically based on predefined conditions (such as price, volume, time, etc.), and it is commonly employed by financial institutions and large investors for risk management or arbitrage purposes. This approach helps enhance trading speed and reduces the influence of human emotions, allowing for the consistent execution of trading strategies. Program trading can significantly impact market liquidity and volatility, making regulation and monitoring essential. Large-scale program trading can exert rapid shocks on the market, posing a risk of sudden price fluctuations if automatic buying or selling occurs under specific price or market conditions. Consequently, financial authorities in various countries closely monitor the impact of program trading on market stability and implement safeguards like circuit breakers to prevent drastic market fluctuations.

PTC (Propensity to Consume)

PTC is an indicator that represents the proportion of income that households or individuals allocate to consumption, and it is used to assess the intensity of consumption activities in the economy. Consumption propensity can be divided into Average Propensity to Consume (APC) and Marginal Propensity to Consume (MPC). APC indicates the ratio of total consumption to total income, while MPC represents the proportion of additional income that is used for consumption. PTC plays a crucial role in economic growth and the activation of the economy, as an increase in consumption positively impacts the overall economy. Policymakers can formulate policies based on consumption propensity, such as tax reductions or income support, to stimulate consumption and promote economic growth. PTC varies according to consumption habits and economic conditions, making it an important indicator in economic analysis.

PV (Present Value)

PV is the amount obtained by discounting a future sum of money to its value at the present time, and it is a financial concept used to evaluate future cash flows in present terms. The calculation of PV involves applying a discount rate, with a higher discount rate resulting in a lower present value of the future amount. Present value is an important indicator for assessing the economic feasibility of investments, loans, and projects. It helps investors predict the actual value of future returns and make comparisons for decision-making. For example, when the expected returns of a specific project are converted into present value, they can be compared with other investment opportunities, enhancing the efficiency of capital allocation. PV varies according to the discount rate, time period, and cash flow, and is frequently used in long-term financial planning.

PVP (Payment versus Payment)

PVP is a system in foreign exchange transactions that ensures payments between different currencies are executed simultaneously to enhance safety. This system aims to mitigate the risk of payment failure, known as settlement risk, which occurs when one side of the transaction is completed while the other fails. PVP is structured so that the payment for one currency does not occur until the payment for the other currency is confirmed, thereby preventing potential losses during the settlement process. Major financial institutions and central banks frequently use PVP to maintain stability in the foreign exchange market. By ensuring simultaneous payments between currencies, the risk of non-fulfillment by one party is reduced. For example, in a foreign exchange transaction between US dollars and euros, PVP ensures that both dollar and euro payments are executed at the same time, lowering the risk of default by either party. The PVP system has established itself as a crucial tool for managing risks in foreign exchange transactions and enhancing the reliability of international payment systems. Central banks and international financial institutions utilize this system to minimize settlement risks in large-scale foreign exchange transactions, thereby strengthening the overall stability of the financial system.

QE (Qualitative Easing)

QE is a monetary policy in which central banks improve the quality of financial assets as a different approach to stimulate the economy compared to quantitative easing. It primarily focuses on purchasing high-quality assets instead of high-risk assets to enhance the stability of financial markets. This is expected to increase the lending capacity of financial institutions and reduce credit risk across the economy. Qualitative easing targets economic stimulation by focusing on the qualitative improvement of asset composition rather than merely providing liquidity. Central banks typically purchase high-creditrated assets such as government bonds and high-quality corporate bonds, helping financial institutions shift away from high-risk assets to more stable ones. This leads to an overall improvement in the credit environment of the economy, facilitating stable economic growth.

QE (Quantitative Easing)

QE is a non-traditional monetary policy in which central banks provide liquidity to the market through large-scale asset purchases to stimulate the economy. The central bank aims to lower interest rates by purchasing government bonds and other financial assets in bulk, thereby promoting lending and activating consumption and investment. QE is mainly implemented during economic downturns, particularly when interest rates are already low and further reductions are challenging, to increase liquidity and invigorate the economy. Quantitative easing plays a crucial role in facilitating the flow of funds in financial markets and achieving inflation targets to stabilize the economy. However, excessive quantitative easing poses risks of causing long-term inflation or creating asset bubbles, necessitating careful management. QE has been used as a response to financial crises in the United States, Europe, and Japan.

RB (Reserve Base)

RB refers to the currency issued by the central bank, which serves as a foundational asset that directly regulates liquidity in the economy. It consists of the cash circulating in the market and the reserves that banks hold with the central bank, acting as the basic source of liquidity for the economy. The reserve base is adjusted through the central bank's monetary policy, allowing it to influence interest rates and liquidity by varying the supply of reserve base according to economic conditions. The reserve base plays a critical role in supporting the lending and deposit activities of financial institutions and facilitating overall credit creation in the economy. For instance, when the central bank increases the reserve base, commercial banks can lend more funds, potentially stimulating economic activity. Conversely, reducing the supply of reserve base decreases the banks' lending capacity, leading to a contraction in liquidity. Through this economic adjustment function, the reserve base plays a key role in ensuring economic stability and managing inflation.

RCA (Revealed Comparative Advantage)

RCA is an indicator that measures how competitively one country performs in specific goods or services compared to other countries. It is calculated by comparing the share of a particular product in a country's exports with the global market share of that product. This indicator reveals which areas a specific country has a comparative advantage in, making it useful for analyzing trade policies or assessing industrial competitiveness between nations. An RCA value greater than 1 indicates that the country has a comparative advantage in that product, while a value less than 1 suggests the absence of such an advantage. For example, if a country's RCA for the automotive industry is greater than 1, it means that the country is relatively more competitive in the automotive sector. RCA helps in understanding each country's industrial structure and trade patterns, providing critical information for governments and businesses to strategize in the international market. RCA serves as a valuable tool for enhancing economic policy formulation and fostering trade relationships.

RE (Ratchet Effect)

RE refers to the tendency for consumption or prices that have reached a certain level to not easily revert back, but rather to be maintained or increased. It is also known as the "ratchet effect." In economics, this effect often manifests when income rises, leading to an increase in consumption levels; however, when income falls, consumption levels do not easily decrease back to previous levels. As a result, during economic downturns, the reduction in consumption may be limited, and both consumers and businesses may struggle to lower their consumption and costs once they have increased. The ratchet effect influences companies' pricing policies and wage structures, leading to rigidity in cost structures. For instance, when the economy grows and wages increase, it becomes difficult for companies to reduce wages in order to cut costs. Similarly, once product prices are raised due to rising costs, they often do not easily decrease even when costs fall. This ratchet effect can reduce overall flexibility in the economy and limit the ability to respond to economic fluctuations.

REER (Real Effective Exchange Rate)

REER is an exchange rate indicator that compares the value of a country's currency to the currencies of its major trading partners, adjusted for inflation levels. It evaluates actual purchasing power by reflecting not only currency value but also the differences in inflation rates among countries. When the REER rises, it suggests that the relative price of domestic goods becomes more expensive, potentially leading to a decrease in exports; conversely, when it falls, export competitiveness may increase. REER is used to analyze trade competitiveness between countries and serves as an important reference for formulating exchange rate policies and economic strategies. By assessing whether the real value of a country's currency is overvalued or undervalued, countries can predict the impact on trade balances and economic performance.

REITs (Real Estate Investment Trust)

REITs are an investment method that pools funds from multiple investors to invest in various types of real estate and pays out the resulting income in the form of dividends. They invest in a range of properties, including commercial real estate, residential properties, hotels, and hospitals, generating revenue from rental income and capital gains from property sales. REITs allow small investors to participate in real estate investment while providing high liquidity and regular dividends. Additionally, they offer an indirect investment approach that reduces management burdens and diversifies risk through portfolio diversification. REITs are popular among investors seeking stable cash flow and can be easily bought and sold on stock exchanges when publicly listed.

RI (Real Income)

RI refers to income that reflects actual purchasing power by taking into account the price level, meaning it is the nominal income adjusted for the effects of inflation. Real income indicates the quantity of goods and services that a person or household can actually purchase, making it a more accurate measure of living standards. For example, even if income increases, if prices rise more significantly, real income may decrease, leading to reduced purchasing power. RI is an important indicator for evaluating the actual consumption capacity of individuals and households in the economy, essential for assessing living standards and formulating economic policies. It enables policymakers to analyze the impact of inflation on the living standards of citizens and to evaluate whether increases in income genuinely contribute to an improvement in quality of life. Understanding real income is crucial for ensuring that economic growth translates into tangible benefits for the population.

RML (Reverse Mortgage Loan)

RML is a financial product that allows seniors to borrow a certain amount of money from a financial institution using their owned home as collateral, providing assistance in funding living expenses or healthcare costs during retirement. The borrower can live in the home while retaining ownership, and repayment typically occurs when the borrower passes away or sells the house. Reverse mortgages offer economic liquidity to elderly individuals who have assets but lack cash flow, while also helping them maintain housing stability. This option is popular among seniors looking to secure retirement funds based on rising home values or stable home ownership, and in some countries, the government guarantees the loans to enhance their security.

ROA (Return on Asset)

ROA is a financial metric that evaluates how efficiently a company generates profit by utilizing its assets. It is calculated by dividing net income by total assets, reflecting the efficiency of asset utilization. A high ROA indicates that a company is effectively managing its assets to generate profits, while a low ROA may suggest inefficiencies in asset use. ROA serves as an important benchmark for management and investors to compare and assess a company's asset efficiency. It can help identify ways to enhance asset utilization and improve profitability. The ideal ROA level varies by industry, so it is crucial to conduct relative evaluations within the same sector when comparing different companies.

ROE (Return on Equity)

ROE is a metric that indicates how efficiently a company generates profit using shareholders' invested capital. It is calculated by dividing net income by shareholders' equity, showing how effectively the capital invested by shareholders is converted into profits. This metric plays a crucial role in assessing a company's management efficiency and shareholder value; generally, a higher ROE signifies that a company is effectively utilizing shareholders' capital. ROE is a key indicator for company management and investors to evaluate profitability and financial performance. A high ROE suggests that shareholders' capital is being used effectively, which can serve as a positive signal for the company's management efficiency and growth potential. Conversely, a low ROE indicates lower profitability relative to shareholders' equity, which may suggest issues with cost structure or inefficiencies in asset utilization.

ROI (Return on Investment)

ROI is a metric used to assess the profit generated relative to the capital invested, measuring the efficiency of an investment. It is expressed as a percentage by dividing net profit by the investment cost. A high ROI indicates that substantial profits have been generated with relatively low investment, making it a valuable tool for evaluating investment performance and making funding allocation decisions. ROI helps management and investors compare the profitability of various investment options and optimize capital allocation. For instance, by using ROI, one can evaluate the performance of multiple projects or assets, seeking the most efficient use of resources.

ROR (Return on Revenue)

ROR is a metric that indicates the proportion of net income relative to total revenue, demonstrating how efficiently a company generates profit from its sales. It is calculated by dividing net income by total revenue (or sales), with a higher value indicating that the company is effectively maintaining profitability relative to its revenue. ROR plays an important role in assessing a company's operational efficiency and cost management capabilities. It is a useful indicator for evaluating overall profitability and understanding management efficiency. A high ROR signifies that costs are low relative to revenue, indicating efficient cost structure management by the company. Conversely, a low ROR may signal excessive costs compared to revenue or difficulties in generating profit relative to sales.

RP (Repurchase Agreements)

RP is a short-term financial transaction in which a security owner borrows funds with the agreement to repurchase the security at a specified price after a certain period. It is primarily used as a funding mechanism among financial institutions, allowing them to secure temporary liquidity through the sale and subsequent repurchase of securities. RP provides a quick way for financial institutions to raise funds when needed. Repurchase agreements are considered low-risk and stable instruments for short-term fund management, also serving as a tool for central banks in their monetary policy operations. This mechanism plays a significant role in regulating liquidity in financial markets and influencing interest rates. RP transactions frequently occur between financial institutions, as they provide collateral for lenders and offer borrowers the advantage of accessing funds for a short duration.

RPS (Retail Payment System)

RPS is a payment system used to process everyday small transactions, facilitating interactions between individuals and retailers. It encompasses various payment methods such as credit cards, debit cards, mobile payments, and e-wallets, designed to complete transactions quickly and securely. This system is commonly used by individual consumers and retailers, promoting consumption activities within the economy. RPS efficiently supports the transfer of funds between consumers and retailers through connections with financial institutions and payment networks, ensuring smooth capital flow in the economy. The stability and speed of RPS are essential for the growth of e-commerce and digital payment methods, and it is evolving to support an increasingly diverse range of payment options through financial innovation.

RSF (Required Stable Funding)

RSF refers to the minimum amount of stable funding required for financial institutions to safely maintain their assets and external exposures. It indicates the amount of funding needed to ensure that the institution can operate stably, particularly to secure adequate funding for long-term assets. This helps financial institutions respond to short-term funding outflows or liquidity crises and plays a crucial role in ensuring the stability of their long-term funding structure. RSF primarily functions to reduce risk by managing the liquidity and maturity of the institution's assets. Financial institutions calculate the required funding ratio based on the characteristics of each asset and must secure stable funding that matches the maturity of their assets. RSF is a key requirement for the long-term stability of financial institutions as part of the Basel III regulations. To meet the NSFR (Net Stable Funding Ratio) requirement, institutions must compare their RSF with ASF (Available Stable Funding) to maintain stable funding. This approach helps reduce maturity mismatches between assets and liabilities and enhances the overall stability of the financial system.

RT (RegTech, Regulatory Technology)

RT refers to the systems and tools that financial institutions and companies use to comply with legal regulations and manage risks by leveraging advanced technologies. It primarily utilizes technologies such as big data, artificial intelligence (AI), and block chain to automate compliance procedures and enhance efficiency. This enables companies to monitor and analyze data related to legal regulations in real-time, thereby reducing legal risks and compliance costs. RegTech efficiently supports compliance monitoring, risk assessment, and data management for financial institutions in response to complex regulatory environments. By using RegTech, financial institutions can swiftly adapt to regulatory changes, playing a crucial role in maintaining financial stability and preventing legal violations. RegTech is especially valuable in the heavily regulated financial sector, promoting digital innovation in regulatory compliance.

RWA (Risk-Weighted Assets)

RWA refers to the size of a financial institution's assets adjusted for the risk associated with each asset. Financial institutions, such as banks, calculate RWA by applying risk weights assigned to different assets, which are used to assess capital requirements and regulatory compliance. For example, safe assets like government bonds are assigned low risk weights, while riskier assets such as loans receive higher weights. RWA serves as the foundational data for calculating a bank's capital ratios and managing risk. Financial institutions must calculate their capital adequacy ratio based on RWA to meet capital requirements set by regulatory authorities. According to Basel III regulations, institutions are required to hold more capital against higher-risk assets, ensuring that they maintain a stable capital structure capable of absorbing unexpected losses.

S&P (Standard & Poor)

S&P is a financial services company renowned for its credit rating evaluations and index calculations in the global financial markets. It assesses the creditworthiness of corporations, countries, and financial products, helping investors understand the credit risks associated with borrowers. Credit ratings are classified from AAA to D, and these evaluations serve as a reference for financial institutions and investors when making investment decisions. Additionally, S&P produces various indices that reflect the stock market, with the S&P 500 index being the most famous. The S&P 500 index is based on the stock prices of 500 major U.S. companies and is used as a key indicator to understand the overall trends in the U.S. economy and stock market. The ratings and indices provided by S&P are trusted sources of information in the global financial market.

SAP (System Application and Programs in Data Process)

SAP is software that supports enterprise resource planning and business operations, serving as a leading provider of ERP (Enterprise Resource Planning) systems. It enables various departments within a company, such as finance, human resources, logistics, and production, to share data and process tasks in real-time within an integrated system. This enhances operational efficiency and maintains data accuracy. The SAP system supports the decision-making process of companies through large-scale data processing and integration, making it widely used globally. SAP's modules are designed to meet the needs of various industries, providing customized solutions and facilitating the standardization and automation of business processes. SAP plays a crucial role in enhancing a company's competitiveness and has established itself as a representative provider of ERP solutions in the global market.

SAS (Statistical Analysis System)

SAS is software that performs data analysis, statistical processing, and predictive modeling, serving as a powerful tool for big data and business intelligence. It handles the entire process from data collection to analysis and visualization, and is utilized in various industries for statistical analysis and data-driven decision-making. This allows companies and research institutions to make strategic decisions based on accurate data analysis. SAS provides advanced analytical capabilities, including statistical analysis, machine learning, and data mining, helping to systematically understand and predict data in research and business environments. It is particularly used in fields where large-scale data management and analysis are critical, such as finance, healthcare, and manufacturing, offering practical insights by identifying patterns and trends in data. SAS has established itself as an essential analytical tool among data science and analytics professionals.

SB (Specialized Banking)
SB refers to a financial service that focuses on specific financial services or customer groups. Unlike general banks that offer a wide range of financial services, specialized banks concentrate on particular industries, sizes of enterprises, or types of customers (e.g., small and medium-sized enterprises, agriculture) to provide tailored financial services. Examples include agricultural banks and banks specializing in loans for small businesses. Specialized banking has the advantage of offering deep understanding and customized financial solutions for specific needs, thereby enhancing competitiveness within the industry. As a result, it plays a crucial role in providing differentiated services in the financial market and supporting the growth of specific sectors.

SB (Straight Bond)
SB refers to a basic form of bond that has a fixed interest rate and maturity date without any specific options. This type of bond pays a

fixed interest (coupon) regularly, and repays the principal amount at maturity, allowing investors to expect stable returns without volatility. These bonds are simple, lacking any additional conversion options or early redemption rights, making them a preferred choice for stable investment. They provide investors with fixed income and are considered the most basic and straightforward form of bonds in the bond market. Issued by corporations or governments to raise funds, the yield on these bonds is determined by their credit quality. SBs are particularly attractive to investors seeking stable income, as they carry less risk compared to other forms of bonds.

SC (Sunk Cost)

SC refers to costs that have already been incurred and cannot be recovered, and they are considered irrelevant to future decision-making. These costs arise from past investments or expenditures, and whether a project is abandoned or continued, they cannot be recouped. Examples of sunk costs include research and development expenses, advertising costs, and equipment installation costs, which should not be factored into further decision-making since they have already been spent. Sunk costs can exert an irrational influence on decision-making, leading individuals to persist in a project even if it results in a loss, due to the psychological tendency to avoid wasting past investments. This phenomenon is known as the "Sunk Cost Fallacy," and economics advises ignoring sunk costs, focusing instead on future expected revenues and costs. For instance, a company should not continue a low-profit project simply because it has made significant initial investments.

SC (Supplementary Capital)

SC refers to the additional capital that financial institutions hold beyond their core capital to meet capital regulations. This capital is primarily established to enhance the stability of financial institutions and provide financial resilience against sudden losses. Supplementary capital typically carries higher risks or has lower recoverability compared to Tier 1 Capital but plays a crucial role in fulfilling regulatory capital requirements. This capital includes subordinated debt, certain forms of convertible bonds, and long-term borrowings, assisting financial institutions in withstanding unexpected losses and maintaining normal operations. Supplementary capital is particularly vital in times of financial crises, contributing to the stability of the financial system and the protection of customer assets. According to Basel regulations, financial institutions must maintain sufficient core and supplementary capital relative to their assets to ensure long-term financial stability. Supplementary capital complements core capital, helping financial institutions manage risk and enhance their resilience during economic downturns or crises.

SCF (Sunk Cost Fallacy)

SCF refers to the psychological error of making irrational decisions based on costs that have already been incurred and cannot be recovered (sunk costs). It reflects the tendency to continue investing in a project or endeavor due to the regret of previous investments of time, effort, or money, even in inefficient situations. For instance, if a time-consuming project is likely to fail, the inclination to proceed simply because of prior investments exemplifies the sunk cost fallacy. This error can obstruct rational decision-making and lead to inefficient resource wastage, making it crucial to be aware of its effects. To overcome the sunk cost fallacy, it is important to disregard past expenditures and focus on future benefits and costs. In economics and management, avoiding this fallacy and not considering sunk costs is emphasized to facilitate efficient resource allocation. Recognizing and mitigating the impact of the sunk cost fallacy is essential for making sound decisions that enhance overall efficiency and effectiveness.

SCM (Supply Chain Management)

SCM refers to a strategic approach to efficiently managing the entire process through which products or services move from the raw material stage to the final consumer. It encompasses materials procurement, production, logistics, inventory management, and distribution, aiming to reduce costs and enhance quality at each stage of the supply chain. This enables companies to ensure a fast and reliable supply to their customers. SCM plays a crucial role in enhancing a company's competitiveness and improving customer satisfaction. By optimizing each component of the supply chain, it helps reduce costs and respond flexibly to changing demands. In today's global market, effectively managing complex supply chains is essential, allowing companies to quickly adapt to market changes and risks.

SDR (Special Drawing Rights)

SDR is an artificial international reserve asset issued by the International Monetary Fund (IMF) to enhance international liquidity and support exchange rate stability among member countries. It is calculated based on a weighted basket of major currencies such as the dollar, euro, yuan, yen, and pound, rather than a specific currency. IMF member countries can hold SDRs and exchange them for foreign currency as needed. SDRs serve as a vital means of bolstering international liquidity and allowing member countries to access IMF funds during economic crises or foreign exchange shortages. They help to adjust trade imbalances between nations and contribute to maintaining trust in international financial markets. SDRs are primarily used among central banks and international financial institutions and serve as a unique asset within the IMF, distinct from conventional currencies.

SE (Snob Effect)

SE refers to a consumer behavior where individuals find greater appeal in products as their prices increase, particularly evident in high-priced goods that emphasize scarcity. Through the snob effect, consumers aim for differentiated consumption, believing that high prices or prestigious brands symbolize their social status. For example, the demand for luxury goods or limited-edition products exemplifies this consumption pattern. The snob effect is characterized by purchasing decisions being influenced more by price and scarcity rather than the quality of the product, impacting brand strategy and pricing decisions. This effect is primarily leveraged in the luxury market, where product scarcity and high pricing strategies stimulate consumer purchasing psychology and enhance the brand's value.

SEEA (System of Integrated Environmental and Economic Accounts)

The SEEA is an international statistical framework developed to systematically measure the interactions between the natural environment and economic activities. It quantifies the impact of economic activities on the environment and resource usage, supporting decision-making for sustainable economic growth. This system integrates environmental assets (such as water, forests, and land) and the flows of energy and waste to analyze the interconnections between the environment and the economy. SEEA provides essential information for formulating environmental policies and managing resources sustainably, helping to maintain a balance between economic growth and environmental conservation. Through this framework, governments and international organizations can develop policies based on environmental and economic data, aiming to achieve long-term environmental protection alongside economic prosperity. The SEEA is primarily developed by the United Nations Statistics Division and is used as a standard for environmental economic statistics in various countries.

SF (Settlement Finality)

SF refers to the state in which a financial transaction is completed and becomes irreversible. It is primarily used in payment systems to ensure that a specific transaction is legally finalized within the system, meaning that it cannot be altered or canceled afterward. This is a critical element that allows transaction parties to mitigate the risks associated with transactions and ensures the certainty of fund transfers. Settlement finality plays an important role in enhancing the stability and reliability of the financial system. Particularly, when a transaction is finalized with legal validity within the payment system, the parties involved can utilize their assets without worrying about the risk of cancellation. This principle ensures that transactions can be processed securely, even in the event of financial crises or system errors, making it essential for financial institutions to manage transaction risks effectively.

SI (Social Insurance)

SI refers to an insurance system operated by the government to protect citizens from risks associated with illness, unemployment, old age, and disability. It provides financial support when individuals experience income loss or economic hardship, contributing to the health and stability of the population. Representative forms of social insurance include health insurance, unemployment insurance, pension insurance, and workers' compensation insurance, most of which are mandatory, serving as a social safety net. Social insurance is operated by collecting contributions from individuals and businesses in the form of premiums, which are then used to provide benefits when needed.

SIFIs (Systemically Important Financial Institutions)

SIFIs refer to financial institutions whose failure or significant losses could have a serious impact on the overall financial system. This category includes major global banks, large insurance companies, and key financial network providers, all of which play a crucial role in economic stability. Systemically important financial institutions hold large assets and account for significant portions of financial markets, meaning their failure could trigger a chain reaction in the financial system. To prevent this, SIFIs are subject to stricter capital requirements, liquidity standards, and regulatory oversight than ordinary financial institutions, and rapid intervention measures are put in place during financial crises. International organizations and regulatory authorities in various countries have established special management frameworks to reduce the risks associated with SIFIs and maintain the stability of the financial system.

SIO (Stock Index Options)

SIO are options contracts that have a specific stock index as the underlying asset, allowing investors to trade rights related to future price fluctuations of the index. They are categorized into call options (buying rights) and put options (selling rights), granting the investor the right to buy or sell the stock index at a specific price on the expiration date of the option. This allows investors to seek profits based on the rise or fall of the stock index. Stock index options are frequently used for risk management in portfolios and serve as a hedging tool against overall market volatility. For example, an investor may purchase put options to protect against the risk of falling stock prices or call options to adjust risk in anticipation of a price increase. SIOs are valuable tools not only for individual investors but also for institutional investors, aiding in volatility management and investment strategy formulation.

SM (Secondary Market)

SM refers to the market where previously issued financial assets, such as stocks and bonds, are traded between investors. Unlike the primary market, where corporations or governments initially raise funds, the secondary market operates through the transfer of ownership of existing assets among investors. Secondary markets, like stock exchanges, enhance the liquidity of assets and provide an environment where investors can easily buy or sell assets when needed. This market offers investors opportunities to convert assets into cash and facilitates liquidity and price discovery. For instance, if an investor buys shares of a particular company in the primary market, they can sell those shares to another investor in the secondary market. The prices formed in the secondary market are determined by supply and demand and fluctuate based on various factors, including the performance of the issuing company or entity and economic conditions, thereby reflecting the fair market value of the assets. By allowing investors to freely buy and sell assets, the secondary market plays a crucial role in enhancing the efficiency of financial markets. With an active secondary market, investors can diversify investment risks or restructure their assets as needed. A wide range of financial assets, including stocks, bonds, derivatives, and ETFs, are traded in the secondary market, contributing to the liquidity and stability of the financial system.

SNA (System of National Accounts)

SNA is an international standard statistical system designed to systematically record and analyze a country's economic activities. It measures economic activities such as production, consumption, investment, and trade, and is used to derive key economic indicators like GDP (Gross Domestic Product). This system helps to understand the size, structure, and growth rate of the national economy while providing essential data for economic policy formulation and international comparisons. Developed and endorsed by international organizations such as the United Nations, World Bank, and IMF, the SNA is designed to enable countries to analyze and report their economies using standardized criteria. This facilitates comparisons of economic data between nations and plays a critical role in evaluating economic performance and establishing sustainable growth policies.

SO (Smoothing Operation)

SO refers to the process of reducing the volatility of data or graphs to derive more consistent patterns. It helps to remove noise or irregularities, making it easier to identify the overall trend of the data and is used in various fields such as financial market analysis, economic data processing, and demand forecasting. By smoothing out complex data, key trends can be more clearly observed. Various techniques such as moving averages and exponential smoothing are employed, which are useful for analyses that prioritize long-term trends over short-term fluctuations. For example, smoothing short-term stock price fluctuations allows for easier identification of long-term price trends, aiding in investment strategy formulation. Similarly, reducing the volatility of economic indicators can provide clearer data for making policy decisions. SO is a crucial process that enhances the efficiency of data analysis and adds reliability to decision-making. By identifying consistent patterns and eliminating noise, analysts can improve the accuracy of trend analysis and forecasting, playing an important role in various decision-making scenarios, including demand forecasting, economic policy assessment, and long-term strategy development in financial markets.

SO (Stock Option)

SO is a financial contract that grants the holder the right to purchase company shares at a predetermined price within a specified period. It is primarily offered as an incentive to employees, encouraging them to feel a sense of responsibility towards the company's growth and performance while allowing them to share in the benefits of an increase in stock price. When the market price of the stock rises above the option exercise price, the option holder can profit. Stock options serve as a motivational tool to promote the company's performance and increase in stock value, encouraging long-term contributions from employees.

SOHO (Small Office Home Office)

SOHO refers to a business model operated in small office or home office environments, primarily involving small business owners, freelancers, and remote workers. This model allows businesses to operate in smaller spaces rather than large offices, and it has become increasingly popular due to advancements in internet and digital technology. The concept has become commonplace across many industries, especially with the expansion of telecommuting, remote work, and small startups. SOHO enables business operations with low initial costs and high flexibility, making it particularly advantageous during the early stages of a startup or when cost reduction is necessary. Small offices allow businesses to operate without the burden of large office rentals or operational costs, and setting up a home office can reduce commuting time and increase efficiency. This operational approach is particularly suitable for those engaged in technology and online businesses.

SP (Sterilization Policy)

SP refers to the monetary policy implemented by central banks to

minimize the impact of liquidity changes on the domestic economy
caused by interventions in the foreign exchange market. When a
central bank buys or sells foreign currency to stabilize the exchange
rate, the supply of its domestic currency may change. To offset this
effect, the central bank adjusts the money supply through open
market operations. The sterilization policy aims to achieve both
exchange rate stability and price stability, typically used by countries
with trade surpluses or high capital inflows. By doing so, the central
bank can control monetary expansion or contraction and maintain the
macroeconomic stability of its economy.

SR (Swap Rate)

SR refers to the fixed interest rate in an interest rate swap agreement,
where one party pays a fixed rate and the other pays a floating rate.
The swap rate is primarily utilized by companies and financial
institutions to manage interest rate risk on long-term loans or to
reduce borrowing costs. In a swap transaction, the fixed rate is
determined based on market interest rates and can be exchanged for
a floating rate to manage the risks associated with interest rate
fluctuations. The swap rate is a key component of interest rate swap
contracts, used by lenders and borrowers to adjust interest rate risk
and optimize financial costs. This is particularly useful when
predicting interest rate changes over the long term is challenging,
allowing for reduced risk through the exchange of fixed and floating
rates and enabling stable fund management.

ST (Security Thread)

ST refers to a thin strip made of metal or plastic embedded in
banknotes or important documents to prevent counterfeiting. It is
often integrated into the paper material of the banknote in a thread-
like manner or printed on the surface, and it can be easily identified

by the naked eye or by shining light at specific angles. The security thread is one of the anti-counterfeiting technologies that adds unique features and authentication elements to help verify the authenticity of banknotes. It is widely used to enhance the reliability of banknotes issued by central banks and to prevent counterfeiting activities. Security threads often include micro-printing or reflective coatings and can be designed to display various color changes when exposed to light. Especially in high-denomination banknotes or important documents, security threads are effective in preventing counterfeiting while being easily identifiable.

ST (Stress Test)

ST refers to a test that evaluates how well financial institutions can withstand simulated economic shocks or crisis situations. Various scenarios, such as economic recessions, sharp interest rate hikes, and stock market crashes, are set up to assess the financial stability and resilience of the institutions. Through this process, financial institutions can prepare for unexpected market fluctuations and risks, and, if necessary, strengthen their capital or risk management strategies. Stress testing is a key tool for assessing the soundness of financial institutions and reducing systemic risk. Following the global financial crisis, central banks and financial regulatory agencies in various countries regularly conduct stress tests to identify vulnerabilities in the financial system in advance and manage potential risks. For example, banks establish capital requirements for different scenarios to prepare for possible loan defaults or capital shortages during hypothetical economic crises, and they develop response plans accordingly.

SU (Statistical Underground)

SU refers to informal or undisclosed economic activities that are not included in official statistics, leading to their omission in economic analysis. This typically comprises informal labor, tax evasion, and illegal economic activities, which, when not reflected in official statistics, can result in an inaccurate representation of the actual economy's size and performance. This absence of data can hinder policymakers and economists from understanding the overall economy, potentially diminishing the effectiveness of economic policies. It distorts the real size and structure of the economy and can pose challenges for accurate policy formulation. For instance, some self-employed individuals or small businesses may prefer informal transactions to avoid reporting income or evading taxes. Since these economic activities are not captured in statistics, the government may struggle to grasp the economic situation accurately, making it difficult to formulate sound fiscal and social policies.

SUT (Supply and Use Tables)

SUT is a statistical table that records and analyzes the flow of production, distribution, and consumption of goods and services within a country's economy. It systematically illustrates how goods and services are produced and used across various industrial sectors, aiding in understanding the flow of economic activities such as production, imports, consumption, exports, and investment. SUT serves as a crucial resource for comprehending the overall structure of national production and expenditure. It is connected to the System of National Accounts (SNA), playing an essential role in deriving economic indicators like GDP and analyzing the economic structure. By showcasing all economic activities from the production stage to final consumption, SUT allows for an understanding of interrelationships between sectors and the industrial structure. This enables policymakers to assess the overall structure of the economy and the efficiency of resource allocation, facilitating the design of necessary economic policies.

SWIFT (Society of Worldwide Interbank Financial Telecommunication)

SWIFT is a system that provides a standardized financial messaging network, enabling safe and rapid fund transfers between banks and financial institutions internationally. Through this network, financial institutions can send and receive financial messages for remittances, foreign exchange transactions, and securities transactions in a unified message format from anywhere in the world. SWIFT has established itself as an internationally recognized standard for financial communication, with thousands of financial institutions relying on this system to support fast and efficient international financial transactions. The SWIFT system ensures the safety and efficiency of interbank remittances, facilitating the smooth operation of the global financial system. Each financial institution is assigned a unique identification code, which allows for the accurate designation of banks during international transfers. This standardized approach reduces errors that may occur during the fund transfer process, enhances the speed of remittances, and improves security.

TB (Trading Book)

TB refers to the portfolio of financial assets held by financial institutions for the purpose of generating short-term trading profits. This portfolio includes various financial instruments such as stocks, bonds, and derivatives, which are traded or liquidated quickly in response to market fluctuations. Since these assets are exposed to market risk and credit risk, financial institutions aim to evaluate and manage them swiftly to minimize potential losses. Unlike general investment portfolios, the trading book focuses on short-term trading strategies to capitalize on price differences. To achieve this, financial institutions frequently assess the assets in the trading book and

actively manage transactions according to market conditions. In
accordance with international financial regulatory standards, the
assets in the trading book are revalued daily based on market prices,
and due to the higher risks involved, regulators impose stricter capital
requirements on trading books.

TDE (Trickle-Down Effect)

TDE is an economic theory that suggests that even if the benefits of
economic growth and wealth are concentrated among the upper class,
over time, these benefits will trickle down to the middle and lower
classes, positively impacting the overall economy. This theory is
primarily based on the assumption that policies such as tax cuts for
the wealthy and support for businesses will eventually create jobs and
increase wages, thereby benefiting lower-income groups as well.
While the trickle-down effect is often used as a rationale for policies
aimed at stimulating economic growth, it is a subject of controversy.
Critics argue that wealth generated at the top does not necessarily
spread to the middle and lower classes, which can exacerbate income
inequality. Some economists advocate for direct benefits to the middle
and lower classes, arguing that this approach is more effective. In
contrast to the trickle-down effect is the Fountain Effect, which posits
that supporting low-income and middle-class individuals can
stimulate economic growth. This theory suggests that strengthening
the purchasing power of these groups can lead to positive spillover
effects across the economy. The Fountain Effect aims to create a
virtuous cycle in which increased consumption from lower-income
and middle-class households boosts corporate revenues and
employment, invigorating the overall economy.

TFR (Total Fertility Rate)

TFR is a measure that indicates the average number of children a woman is expected to have during her reproductive years (ages 15 to 49). It is an important indicator used to predict population growth rates and future demographic structures, often employed in the formulation of population policies and the assessment of social changes in a country or region. A TFR of 2.1 or higher is considered necessary for a population to maintain itself, while a rate below this suggests a potential decline in population. TFR is influenced by various factors, including socioeconomic conditions, education levels, women's participation in the workforce, and access to healthcare services. For instance, rising living costs, housing insecurity, and the financial burden of raising children tend to lower the TFR. This decline can lead to long-term issues such as labor shortages and an aging population, prompting many countries to implement policies aimed at increasing birth rates.

TiVA (Trade in Value Added)

TiVA is an indicator that measures the portion of value added that is actually created in each country's exports and imports, allowing for the analysis of trade flows. Traditional trade statistics are calculated based on the total value of finished products; however, TiVA tracks the value added at each stage of production to identify the actual economic contributions of each country to trade. This approach clarifies the economic contributions made by specific countries within the Global Value Chain (GVC). As global value chains become more complex, TiVA addresses the limitations of traditional trade statistics and is useful for more accurately assessing the trade dependence and competitiveness of countries. For example, if a country imports intermediate goods, assembles them, and then exports the final product, TiVA considers only the value added by that country as its trade contribution. This provides important information for more accurately analyzing trade imbalances between countries and the contributions of various industries.

TRS (Total Return Swap)

TRS is a derivative transaction in which the total return of an asset (including interest, dividends, and capital gains) is exchanged between two parties. One party receives the total return of a specific asset (such as stocks, bonds, or real estate) while paying a fixed or floating interest rate to the other party. Conversely, the other party receives the agreed-upon interest while providing the total return of the asset. This allows for the opportunity to earn returns without holding the asset or to hedge the risks associated with the asset. TRS enables financial institutions and investors to participate in the returns and risks of an asset without directly owning it, offering investment opportunities through leverage. For example, an investor wanting to receive the total return of a specific bond can use a TRS to gain returns without directly purchasing the bond, thereby reducing the risk of asset ownership and lowering capital costs.

TSR (Total Share Return)

TSR is a metric that measures the total return received by shareholders over a specific period, including stock price appreciation and dividend income. It encompasses all benefits received by shareholders, such as capital gains from stock price increases, dividends, and stock splits, to evaluate the actual investment performance experienced by shareholders. This makes TSR a crucial tool for assessing a company's profitability and shareholder value. Since TSR reflects both the stock price increase and the dividend yield, it provides a comprehensive view of total investment performance that cannot be captured by stock price changes alone. For example, if a stock appreciates by 5% over a year and pays a dividend yield of 3%, the TSR would be 8%. This figure considers not only capital gains but also the income generated through dividends, offering a more realistic representation of total shareholder returns. TSR is frequently used as a benchmark for evaluating a company's long-term ability to create shareholder value and for comparing investment performance.

TUE (Trickle-Up Effect)

TUE is an economic theory that suggests that support for low-income and middle-class individuals and the stimulation of their consumption can lead to overall economic growth. By increasing the purchasing power of lower-income groups, consumer demand expands, resulting in positive spillover effects such as increased sales for businesses and job creation throughout the economy. In other words, the rise in consumption among lower-income groups benefits higher-income individuals and companies, promoting economic growth across the board. The trickle-up effect argues that direct support and wage increases for low-income and middle-class individuals can serve as a foundation for economic growth and contribute to alleviating social inequality. For example, policies aimed at providing living cost support, and expanding access to education and healthcare can foster economic stability for low-income individuals, allowing them to increase their consumption and invigorate the entire economy.

UB (Universal Banking)

UB refers to a banking model in which a single financial institution offers both commercial and investment banking functions. This model provides a wide range of financial services, including traditional deposit and loan operations, securities issuance, asset management, insurance, and investment advisory services, all under one roof to comprehensively meet the financial needs of customers. This convenience allows customers to receive a full suite of services without the need to visit multiple financial institutions. Universal banking enables financial institutions to diversify their revenue sources and spread risks through business diversification. For instance, if interest income from loans decreases, the revenue generated from securities investments or asset management services can compensate for that loss. The universal banking model enhances operational efficiency and achieves economies of scale by allowing large financial institutions to provide a variety of financial services in an integrated manner. However, this model also exposes institutions to various risks and raises the potential for conflicts of interest due to the combination of investment and commercial activities.

UE (Underground Economy)

UE refers to informal economic activities that occur outside government regulation or as a means to evade taxes. This includes unreported income for tax evasion, illegal transactions, and unlicensed operations, which are not reflected in official economic statistics and can distort the actual size of the economy. The underground economy can lead to a shortage of government revenue and poses a risk to the legitimate market order. Since the income generated in the underground economy is unreported, governments struggle to establish accurate fiscal policies. For example, some self-employed individuals or freelancers may conduct transactions in cash without reporting their income or evade taxes through illegal goods trading. The underground economy undermines economic transparency and can exacerbate social inequality. As the size of the underground economy increases, the tax base weakens, making it difficult for the government to support public services or welfare policies. To prevent this, various countries are implementing policies to curb the underground economy and are making efforts to enhance the transparency of economic activities.

USDI (US Dollar Index)

USDI measures the value of the US dollar relative to six major currencies. This index uses a weighted average of six currencies, including the euro, yen, pound, Canadian dollar, Swedish krona, and Swiss franc, to assess the relative strength and weakness of the dollar. Established with a base value of 100 in 1973, the USDI indicates the fluctuations of the dollar over time, providing a clear view of whether the dollar is strong or weak against other major currencies. The USDI serves as a key indicator for understanding global economic and financial market trends, particularly in assessing the impacts of the dollar's strength or weakness on commodities, foreign exchange, and stock markets. For instance, when the dollar index rises, it indicates a stronger dollar, which may lead to decreased exports and falling commodity prices. Conversely, a decline in the index suggests a weaker dollar, potentially resulting in increased exports and other positive effects.

VAIC (Value Added Inducement Coefficients)

VAIC is an indicator that measures the extent to which one industry induces value added in other industries or the overall economy. This coefficient evaluates the spillover effects of the value added generated by a specific industry on other sectors, providing insight into the contributions of particular sectors to the national economy. VAIC is used to analyze the interconnections between industries and assess the impact of specific sectors on overall economic growth. For example, a high VAIC for the manufacturing sector indicates that this industry significantly contributes economic value to other sectors, suggesting a strong potential for overall value added growth in the economy. Such analysis aids policymakers in developing strategies to support key industries or invest in specific sectors. The value added inducement coefficient is an important metric for analyzing economic structures and formulating industrial policies. It enables governments and businesses to enhance resource allocation efficiency and maximize the positive spillover effects of growth in specific industries on the broader economy.

VAR (Value at Risk)

VAR is a risk management metric that estimates the maximum expected loss of a financial asset over a specified period at a certain confidence level. For instance, if the VAR for a day is 1 billion won at a 95% confidence level, it implies that there is a 5% probability that the loss will exceed 1 billion won within that day. VAR provides essential information for financial institutions and investors to assess the potential losses of a portfolio and develop risk management plans. It quantifies the possibility of loss in financial risk management and is used in investment decision-making. This metric applies to various risk factors, including investment portfolios, market risk, and credit risk, and is particularly useful for a comprehensive evaluation of overall portfolio risk. It serves as a basis for assessing whether financial institutions meet capital holding requirements and for developing strategies to mitigate risk. VAR has established itself as a standard risk assessment tool due to its simplicity and ease of understanding. However, VAR may have limitations in extreme market conditions (tail risk), which often leads to the use of additional risk management metrics, such as CVaR (Conditional Value at Risk), to supplement it.

VC (Virtual Currency)

VC refers to a form of digital currency that exists in a digital format and is traded without being issued by a central bank or government. It is primarily used on the internet and operates through transactions conducted via decentralized ledger technologies, such as blockchain, without the control of a central authority. Prominent examples include Bitcoin and Ethereum, which are secured through cryptographic techniques and operate in a decentralized manner. Virtual currencies are used for various purposes, including payments, remittances, and investments, and are recognized as a form of financial innovation. Unlike traditional currencies, virtual currencies facilitate peer-to-peer (P2P) transactions without regard to borders, making them useful for international remittances and small payments. Additionally, virtual currencies often have inflation-resistant features, as their supply can be limited or adjusted according to specific algorithms.

VE (Veblen's Effect)

VE refers to the phenomenon where consumer demand for certain goods increases as prices rise. This effect stems from the tendency to consume high-priced luxury items or status symbols to demonstrate social status or prestige. It contradicts the basic law of demand, as consumers perceive that expensive products enhance their social standing, leading higher prices to positively influence their purchasing decisions. This effect is particularly prominent in the luxury market, where consumers prefer costly and rare products, thereby reinforcing brand value. Companies can leverage the Veblen Effect to establish premium pricing strategies and stimulate consumer desire through marketing activities that enhance product image and demand. Ultimately, this effect assists businesses in setting premium prices and plays a crucial role in building a high-end brand image and customer loyalty.

WACC (Weighted Average Cost of Capital)

WACC refers to the average cost of capital that a company needs to raise, weighted according to its capital structure. It is calculated by averaging the costs of different capital raising methods, such as equity (own capital) and debt (borrowed capital), based on their proportions. WACC serves as the discount rate for making investment decisions. A lower WACC indicates that the company can raise capital more cheaply, while a higher WACC signifies greater capital costs, which can reduce the profitability of the company's investments.

WLG (Wage-Led Growth)

WLG refers to an economic model that promotes domestic consumption through wage increases, making it a key driver of economic growth. When wages rise, households gain greater purchasing power, stimulating the domestic market and leading to increased corporate revenue and production expansion, ultimately resulting in economic growth. This model is particularly effective in economic structures where consumption by low- and middle-income groups plays a crucial role. Wage-led growth seeks to reduce income inequality and promote stable economic growth centered around domestic demand. As wage increases translate into higher consumption, businesses can ramp up production and expand employment, creating a positive feedback loop that further enhances wages. Unlike export-led growth models, wage-led growth increases dependence on domestic markets and helps mitigate economic instability. WLG is closely related to policies aimed at achieving economic balance through job security and income redistribution, such as raising the minimum wage, protecting workers' rights, and expanding employment opportunities, ultimately enhancing household purchasing power and maintaining stable demand throughout the economy, contributing to sustainable growth.

YTM (Yield to Maturity)

YTM refers to the expected annual return on a bond if held until maturity, encompassing all interest income and principal repayment that the investor will receive by that time, considering the bond's current market price. It serves as a critical indicator for assessing the actual profitability of a bond by reflecting not only the coupon rate but also the current market price, remaining term, and interest payment frequency. Yield to maturity provides a basis for comparing yields when bond prices are above or below par. For instance, purchasing a bond below par value results in a YTM that exceeds the coupon rate, while buying it at a higher price yields a lower YTM. Thus, YTM offers investors essential information to accurately evaluate a bond's current market value and its yield until maturity.

Part 2 Business Administration

AMC (Asset Management Company)	177
APM (Asset Performance Management)	177
B2B (Business to Business)	178
B2C (Business to Customer)	178
BCP (Business Continuity Plan)	179
BD (Big Data)	179
BM (Business Model)	180
BMC (Business Model Canvas)	180
BOD (Board of Directors)	181
BPM (Business Process Management)	182
BSC (Balanced Score Card)	182
BSI (Business Survey Index)	183
CAGR (Compound Annual Growth Rate)	183
CDD (Commercial Due Diligence)	184
CFP (Capital Facilities Plan)	184
CRM (Customer Relationship Management)	185
CS (Customer Satisfaction)	185
CSI (Customer Satisfaction Index)	186
CSR (Corporate Social Responsibility)	186

DRP (Distribution Requirement Planning)	187
EAM (Enterprise Asset Management)	187
EAMS (Enterprise Architecture Management System)	188
EC (Electronic Commerce)	188
EC (Executive Committee)	189
ECCS (Enterprise Controlling and Consolidation System)	189
EDI (Electronic Data Interchange)	190
EIS (Executive Information Systems)	190
ERP (Enterprise Resource Planning)	190
ES (Exit Strategy)	191
ESG (Environment Social Governance)	191
ESI (Employee Satisfaction Index)	192
EV (Enterprise Value)	193
FHC (Financial Holdings Company)	193
FI (Financial Investor)	194
FM (Facility Management)	194
FMV (Fair Market Value)	195
FRM (Financial Risk Management)	195
FS (Feasibility Study)	196

GCF (Green Climate Fund)	196
GRI (Global Reporting Initiative)	197
GT (Group Technology)	197
HRD (Human Resources Development)	198
HTBC (Historical Trend Base Change)	198
IA (Information Asymmetry)	199
IP (Intellectual Property)	199
IPO (Initial Public Offering)	200
IPR (Intellectual Property Rights)	200
IR (Investor Relations)	201
ISDS (Investor-State Dispute Settlement)	201
KMS (Knowledge Management System)	202
KPI (Key Performance Indicator)	202
M&A (Mergers & Acquisition)	202
M&O (Monopoly and Oligopoly)	203
MBA (Master of Business Administration)	203
MBO (Management by Objectives)	204
MS (Market Share)	204
NBD (New Business Development)	205

O&M (Operation & Maintenance)	205
OBS (Organizational Breakdown Structure)	206
OC (Opportunity Cost)	206
OMO (Open Market Operation)	207
OR (Operational Risk)	208
PAM (Plant Asset Management)	208
PF (Project Financing)	208
PFV (Project Financing Vehicle)	209
R&D (Research and Development)	209
SI (Strategic Investor)	210
SOW (Share of Wallet)	210
SPC (Special Purpose Company)	211
SPM (Strategic Performance Measurement)	211
SRI (Socially Responsible Investment)	212
SWOT (Strengths, Weaknesses, Opportunities, Threats)	212
TCO (Total Cost of Ownership)	213
VOC (Voice of Customer)	213

AMC (Asset Management Company)

AMC is a financial institution that manages and operates the assets of individuals and institutional investors to generate returns. It invests funds in various investment products, including stocks, bonds, real estate, and derivatives, creating and managing portfolios tailored to the clients' investment goals and risk preferences. AMCs analyze the market through investment professionals and financial analysts to develop optimal investment strategies aimed at maximizing the value of client assets. Asset management companies assist investors in accessing assets or markets that are difficult to invest in directly and provide services for diversification and risk management. For example, individual investors can indirectly invest in various assets managed by the AMC by investing in the company's funds. This helps clients reduce the complexity of asset management and allows them to expect stable and efficient asset growth based on expert analysis and strategies.

APM (Asset Performance Management)

APM is a management system that monitors and optimizes the performance and condition of physical assets owned by a company, maximizing operational efficiency. It manages the performance of physical assets such as facilities, equipment, and infrastructure in real time, helping to reduce unexpected failures or downtime and lower maintenance costs. APM includes features such as predictive maintenance, asset analytics, and risk management to ensure that a company's assets achieve maximum performance. Utilizing data analytics and IoT sensor technology, APM allows for real-time status tracking of assets and enables early detection of potential issues, facilitating preventive measures. APM plays a crucial role in enhancing asset reliability and efficiency, contributing to the overall success of the organization.

B2B (Business to Business)

B2B refers to a transactional model where one business provides products or services to another business. This can be seen in transactions between manufacturers and suppliers for parts, or in cases where software developers offer solutions to companies, encompassing a variety of products and services that support a business's production processes or operations. Unlike B2C (Business to Consumer), which targets individual consumers, B2B is characterized mainly by bulk transactions and customized solutions. B2B transactions play a crucial role in enhancing a company's efficiency and strengthening collaborative relationships across different industries. For example, an automobile manufacturer may establish a B2B relationship with a supplier of parts to ensure a stable supply and maintain production. In B2B transactions, elements such as price negotiations, long-term contracts, and the provision of customized products are important, highlighting the trust and long-term partnerships between businesses.

B2C (Business to Customer)

B2C refers to a transactional model where businesses directly provide products or services to end consumers. This can be seen in online shopping malls, grocery stores, restaurants, and other establishments where companies sell their produced goods or services directly to the final users. With the advancement of e-commerce, B2C transactions occur actively on both offline and online platforms, offering a convenient shopping experience and various payment options. B2C places a strong emphasis on the customer purchasing experience, characterized mainly by small-volume sales and consumer-oriented marketing. Businesses quickly update their products in response to consumer trends and demand changes, and develop marketing strategies that reflect the interests of individual customers. They focus on securing loyal customers and improving customer experiences, particularly through digital marketing, social media, and mobile apps, allowing for direct communication with consumers.

BCP (Business Continuity Plan)

BCP refers to a comprehensive strategy and procedures that prepare a business to continue its core operations in the event of unexpected disasters, incidents, or system disruptions. It is a systematic plan designed to help organizations respond quickly to crises, minimize damage, and return to normal operations as soon as possible. By implementing a BCP, businesses can reduce financial losses caused by operational interruptions and maintain trust with customers. The plan consists of elements such as risk identification, recovery strategies, emergency contact systems, and testing and training, which include the protection of critical data, systems, personnel, and facilities. For example, ensuring business continuity may involve establishing data backup systems, securing alternative work locations, and reallocating the roles of key personnel. Additionally, regularly testing and updating the plan allows businesses to prepare for evolving risk environments.

BD (Big Data)

BD refers to an extensive amount of data that is difficult to process using traditional database management tools, encompassing the collection, storage, and analysis of various forms of data. Typically characterized by the "3 Vs" — Volume (large-scale), Variety (diverse formats), and Velocity (rapid speed) — it has recently expanded to include two additional Vs: Veracity (data reliability) and Value (data value), thus describing it as the "5 Vs." Big Data includes structured and unstructured data generated from sources like social media, sensors, financial transactions, and online activities, with the goal of analyzing it to derive insights. It creates value across various fields when combined with data analytics, artificial intelligence, and machine learning. For example, analyzing customer purchasing patterns can lead to personalized marketing strategies, or in healthcare, Big Data can be utilized to improve efficiency by predicting diseases. It helps businesses accurately identify customer needs and optimize decision-making. Big Data has established itself as a vital resource in business, science, and public services, contributing to data-driven innovation and enhancing competitiveness. The effective use of Big Data plays a crucial role in securing competitive advantages for businesses and addressing social issues, leading to continuous advancements in data storage technologies and analytical methodologies.

BM (Business Model)

BM refers to the concept that defines how a company creates value and generates revenue. It explains how products or services are delivered to customers and how income is generated. Various business models exist, such as subscription models, premium models, and direct sales models, each designed to meet customer needs and ensure sustainable operations. A business model is a system in which key elements like product development, marketing strategies, and revenue structures are organically combined, playing a crucial role in enhancing a company's competitiveness and differentiating it in the market. For example, the SaaS (Software as a Service) model provides software on a subscription basis, generating recurring revenue while fostering customer loyalty. Such models aim to establish relationships with customers, reduce costs, and increase profitability.

BMC (Business Model Canvas)

BMC is a tool that helps visually represent a company's business model and systematically analyze its components. Developed by Alexander Osterwalder and Yves Pigneur, the BMC is designed to break down the business model into nine key elements, making it easy to understand at a glance. This canvas is useful for founders or businesses when they want to refine their ideas and develop or review their business models. The nine key elements of the BMC are as follows:

1) Customer Segments: Target customer groups.
2) Value Propositions: The unique value offered to customers.
3) Channels: Methods for delivering the value proposition to customers.
4) Customer Relationships: Ways to build relationships with customers.
5) Revenue Streams: Methods of generating revenue.
6) Key Resources: Essential resources needed for business operations.
7) Key Activities: Activities necessary for creating value.
8) Key Partners: Key partners needed for collaboration.
9) Cost Structure: Major costs incurred in operations.

BOD (Board of Directors)

BOD is the highest decision-making body of a corporation, responsible for supervising and approving the company's major policies and strategies on behalf of shareholders. The board oversees the activities of the CEO and the management team, establishes the long-term direction of the company, and has the authority to approve significant financial, operational, and personnel-related decisions. The board typically consists of both internal and external directors, with external directors serving the role of independent monitors of the company's management. The primary responsibilities of the board are to supervise the management and maximize shareholder value. To achieve this, the board establishes the company's strategic objectives, evaluates the performance of the management team, and develops policies to protect shareholder interests. Additionally, the board reviews and approves important management decisions, such as major asset sales, mergers, and financing, ensuring the stability and growth potential of the company.

BPM (Business Process Management)

BPM is a management approach that analyzes, designs, executes, and monitors various business processes within an organization to optimize them. Through BPM, companies can eliminate inefficiencies in their operations and improve workflows, thereby enhancing productivity and quality. By systematically managing processes, BPM reduces time and costs while increasing overall operational efficiency. It can be integrated with systems such as ERP and CRM to ensure consistent management across all operations. BPM supports data-driven decision-making and promotes process improvements through automation. With BPM tools, organizations can visualize workflows and identify areas for maximizing efficiency, automating tasks to create value in key business areas like customer management, inventory management, and quality assurance. BPM plays a crucial role in enabling companies to respond swiftly to changing environments, helping maintain competitiveness and increase customer satisfaction.

BSC (Balanced Score Card)

BSC is a strategic planning tool used to evaluate and manage an organization's performance by considering both financial and non-financial indicators in a balanced manner to support the achievement of organizational goals. This tool measures and analyzes performance through four perspectives: financial, customer, internal processes, and learning and growth. The primary objective of the BSC is to clearly communicate the organization's strategy and align the goals of each department and employee with the overall objectives. This allows management to comprehensively assess the organization's performance and gain insights necessary for making strategic decisions.

BSI (Business Survey Index)

BSI is an index that quantifies businesses' perceptions of the current economic situation and future outlook. It is calculated based on survey responses from companies, with a benchmark of 100; a value above 100 indicates that more companies expect an improvement in the economy, while a value below 100 suggests that more companies anticipate a downturn. BSI serves as a valuable resource for understanding economic trends and formulating economic policies. By reflecting the economic outlook of business executives, it aids in predicting overall economic conditions. This allows policymakers and economic analysts to indirectly gauge companies' investment and production plans, which is crucial for future economic response strategies. Additionally, BSI can be categorized by various industries, such as manufacturing and services, enabling a more detailed understanding of the economic conditions in specific sectors.

CAGR (Compound Annual Growth Rate)

CAGR is the annual growth rate of an investment or revenue that is assumed to grow at a constant rate over a specified period. It calculates the growth rate based on the initial and final values, representing the average growth rate over the entire period. This metric is useful for evaluating various financial performances, such as stock, investment portfolios, and sales growth, and it helps to normalize volatility when comparing long-term performance to accurately assess actual growth. CAGR intuitively expresses the profitability of an investment over a period and is used to evaluate long-term performance and forecast future growth. For example, if an asset doubles in value over five years with consistent growth, the CAGR is calculated as if the asset grew at a constant rate each year. CAGR serves as an important indicator for investors and companies to compare performance over a set period and to set growth targets.

CDD (Commercial Due Diligence)

CDD is the process of evaluating the commercial viability and market competitiveness of a target company when reviewing an acquisition or investment. It involves analyzing the company's market position, competitive landscape, customer and supply chain structure, and growth potential to provide the commercial information necessary for investment decision-making. Through this analysis, investors can assess the likelihood of success for the target company in the market and minimize risks. CDD combines market research with financial analysis to gain a detailed understanding of the target company's business model and growth potential. By understanding industry trends and competitors' strategies, it helps evaluate the company's strategic position and forecast future profitability. This essential procedure provides accurate information to investors and acquirers, aiding in objective assessments of investment value and risk.

CFP (Capital Facilities Plan)

CFP is a long-term plan for future facility investments and asset management, encompassing a comprehensive capital budgeting strategy that includes the construction, maintenance, and replacement of major facilities. It aims to allocate the budget efficiently, extend the lifespan of facilities, and ensure that necessary infrastructure and facilities are in place in a timely manner. Through this planning, organizations can secure the required capital facilities to meet future growth and operational needs. CFP plays a crucial role in assessing the condition of capital facilities and future requirements to prioritize projects and develop financial plans. For instance, when a city or company is pursuing long-term infrastructure development, the CFP serves as a foundation for identifying projected costs and timelines for projects and securing necessary funding. CFP is an essential planning tool used for efficient capital utilization and facility management in both the public and private sectors.

CRM (Customer Relationship Management)

CRM refers to the strategies and technologies that companies use to systematically manage and enhance their relationships with customers. It focuses on managing data such as customers' purchase history, interaction records, and preferences to increase customer satisfaction and loyalty. By doing so, businesses can provide personalized marketing, sales, and customer service activities, allowing them to respond more effectively to customer needs. CRM systems assist in predicting customer behavior through data analysis and in designing effective marketing and customer management strategies. By building long-term relationships with customers through CRM, companies can drive revenue growth and improve customer retention rates. This strategy serves as a critical component for businesses to maintain competitiveness and strengthen their position in the market, contributing to sustainable growth through a customer-centric approach.

CS (Customer Satisfaction)

CS refers to the level of satisfaction that customers feel regarding the quality of a product or service and their overall evaluation of the experience. It is based on the gap between consumer expectations and actual experiences, influenced by various factors such as product performance, price, service, and brand image. High customer satisfaction plays a crucial role in fostering customer repurchase intentions, loyalty, and positive word-of-mouth. It is a key determinant of a company's success and sustainability, necessitating continuous improvement in services and product development based on customer feedback. To achieve this, companies need to collect and analyze customer opinions to establish strategies that meet customer needs and expectations. Customer satisfaction has become an important metric for differentiation in market competition.

CSI (Customer Satisfaction Index)

CSI is a metric that quantifies customer satisfaction with a product or service, used to evaluate a company's performance and customer experience. This index is derived from customer surveys, feedback, reviews, and measures the gap between customer expectations and actual experiences to reflect customer satisfaction. A high CSI indicates that customers have a positive perception of the product or service, contributing to increased customer loyalty and repurchase likelihood. CSI serves as a vital tool for companies to understand customer needs and expectations, allowing for reflection in service improvement and product development. By utilizing CSI, companies can continuously monitor customer satisfaction and use it to drive marketing strategies or operational enhancements, thereby strengthening their competitive edge.

CSR (Corporate Social Responsibility)

CSR refers to the voluntary activities that companies undertake to positively impact society and the environment while pursuing economic profits. It involves fulfilling responsibilities to the communities in which they operate, as well as to the environment, employees, customers, and stakeholders, and seeks to promote ethical management and sustainable development. This includes various social initiatives such as environmental protection, community development, and respect for human rights. Corporate social responsibility contributes to building a positive image among consumers and investors, enhancing the long-term sustainability of the business. CSR activities should go beyond mere donations or charitable efforts; they must be integrated into the company's strategy and operations, aligned with the company's values and mission. This plays a crucial role in increasing brand loyalty and building social trust.

DRP (Distribution Requirement Planning)

DRP refers to the process of efficiently managing inventory and planning logistics and distribution based on product demand. This system optimizes inventory levels and establishes distribution strategies by considering sales forecasts and demand fluctuations to ensure that the required inventory is placed in the right locations at the right times.

EAM (Enterprise Asset Management)

EAM is a strategic approach that allows organizations to efficiently manage the lifecycle of their assets to maximize performance and minimize costs. By integrating and managing asset information at every stage—from planning, procurement, and operation to maintenance and disposal—EAM focuses on maximizing asset value and improving operational efficiency. It is essential for optimizing asset operations and maintenance across various industries, including manufacturing, energy, and facilities management. Through EAM, companies can benefit from increased asset uptime, reduced maintenance costs, and performance analysis of assets. EAM solutions enhance management efficiency through data analytics and predictive maintenance capabilities, contributing to the achievement of business goals.

EAMS (Enterprise Architecture Management System)

EAMS is a systematic approach to managing and optimizing an organization's IT systems and business processes in an integrated manner. It defines and aligns information technology and business architecture according to the organization's goals and strategies, contributing to increased efficiency and flexibility. This allows companies to quickly adapt to changing business environments. EAMS encompasses various elements, including resource management, technology standardization, process improvement, and data management, supporting the overall IT strategy of the organization. Through EAMS, organizations can reduce costs and effectively achieve their business objectives. It plays a crucial role in harmonizing IT and business, thereby improving overall organizational performance.

EC (Electronic Commerce)

EC efers to the transaction method of buying and selling goods or services using the internet and digital technologies. This form of commerce encompasses not only transactions between consumers and businesses (B2C) but also transactions between businesses (B2B) and transactions between consumers (C2C). Electronic commerce takes place through shopping websites, online marketplaces, mobile applications, etc., allowing customers to conveniently search for and purchase products. This method enables businesses to reduce operating costs and gain access to a broader market, while providing consumers with a variety of choices and a convenient shopping experience, making it a crucial element of modern commerce.

Furthermore, electronic commerce allows for personalized marketing and customer analysis using data, enabling tailored services that reflect consumer preferences. As a result, businesses can strengthen their relationships with consumers and create a better customer experience.

EC (Executive Committee)

EC is a committee composed of senior executives responsible for making strategic decisions and overseeing major management activities within a company. It plays a crucial role in establishing the company's vision, goals, and policies, as well as developing plans to implement them and directing overall operations. This committee typically includes the CEO and key executives and is central to setting the future direction and strategy of the organization. The Executive Committee analyzes the company's financial performance, market changes, and competitive strategies to share the necessary information for effective decision-making, thereby establishing long-term management strategies. Additionally, the Executive Committee contributes to maintaining transparency in discussions and decision-making processes regarding important management issues and building trust with stakeholders.

ECCS (Enterprise Controlling and Consolidation System)

ECCS is a system designed to integrate financial data across an organization and provide management and reporting functions to assist executives in making better decisions. This system plays a crucial role in monitoring and analyzing the overall financial health of the enterprise, encompassing financial accounting, management accounting, budgeting, and performance analysis. ECCS consolidates financial data from various business segments and regions, enabling the evaluation of overall financial performance and supporting the development of efficient management strategies. Through this integration, the system helps organizations optimize resource allocation and minimize the risks of budget overruns or losses. Additionally, ECCS enhances the accuracy and consistency of data, providing necessary information for regulatory compliance and internal audits.

EDI (Electronic Data Interchange)

EDI refers to the process of exchanging standardized electronic data between businesses. This method allows for the swift and accurate exchange of business information such as purchase orders, invoices, and shipping documents using electronic files instead of paper documents. Electronic Data Interchange enhances the efficiency of logistics and supply chain management, reduces human errors, and shortens processing times.

EIS (Executive Information Systems)

EIS is a system designed to provide executives with quick access to the information necessary to monitor the company's performance and make strategic decisions. It efficiently delivers management information through visualized dashboards, reports, and KPIs, enabling senior executives to easily access and analyze data. EIS automates the processes of data collection, analysis, and reporting, allowing executives to grasp critical business metrics in real time and respond swiftly to market changes. This system provides insights essential for achieving corporate goals and enhances the speed and accuracy of decision-making processes.

ERP (Enterprise Resource Planning)

ERP is a comprehensive software system that integrates and manages various business processes and resources within an organization. It unifies functions such as finance, human resources, production, logistics, and sales, enabling real-time data sharing and analysis. This integration allows companies to enhance efficiency, reduce operational costs, and improve decision-making processes. ERP systems promote collaboration among all departments, maintaining the accuracy and consistency of data to facilitate integrated business operations. For instance, inventory management, production planning, and customer order processing are interconnected, allowing each department to share necessary information in real time, thereby maximizing operational efficiency. ERP has become a crucial tool, particularly for large enterprises, to streamline complex business processes and support sustainable growth.

ES (Exit Strategy)

ES refers to a plan that investors or companies formulate to realize profits from their investments or to terminate a business. It plays a crucial role in managing risks that may arise during the investment process while aiming to achieve maximum returns. Common exit strategies include selling the company, going public, selling equity, and mergers. An exit strategy assists investors and management in achieving long-term business goals and provides a clear direction on how to dispose of investment assets at a planned time. This strategic decision-making capability is vital in uncertain market conditions, helping to maximize profits and reduce management risks. An exit strategy should be considered from the early stages of investment to facilitate successful asset disposal and overall business performance.

ESG (Environment Social Governance)

ESG refers to the three elements that companies should consider for sustainable development: environmental responsibility, social responsibility, and corporate governance. ESG has become a standard for investors and consumers to evaluate non-financial performance, emphasizing the importance of companies fulfilling their social responsibilities and protecting the environment. It is increasingly significant in investment decisions, as companies operating sustainably are perceived to have higher investment value. Through this approach, businesses can build long-term growth and social trust.

1) Environment: This includes the impact of a company's activities on the natural environment, resource management, energy efficiency, and carbon emissions.
2) Social: This addresses labor practices, human rights, relationships with the community, and interactions with customers and suppliers, assessing the company's social responsibility.
3) Governance: This encompasses corporate governance, management transparency, ethical practices, and shareholder protection, evaluating how the company is operated.

ESI (Employee Satisfaction Index)

ESI is a quantitative measure of the overall job satisfaction and work environment perceived by employees within an organization. This index is based on data collected through surveys and feedback, evaluating aspects such as job satisfaction, organizational culture, leadership, and welfare programs. A high ESI indicates that employees have a positive perception of their roles and the organization, which can positively impact productivity and work efficiency. The Employee Satisfaction Index plays a crucial role in attracting and retaining talent, as well as enhancing corporate performance, contributing to the organization's sustainable competitiveness. Companies analyze the ESI to identify areas for improvement and establish policies that align with employee needs and expectations, striving to enhance overall satisfaction. ESI serves as a key indicator in employee management and organizational development strategies.

EV (Enterprise Value)

EV is a metric used to assess a company's total value, reflecting a comprehensive valuation that includes market capitalization, debt, and cash or cash equivalents. It is calculated by adding the company's market capitalization to its net debt. This metric is useful for evaluating a company's total worth, particularly in the context of mergers and acquisitions (M&A) or investment analysis. Enterprise value plays a crucial role in accurately assessing a company's true value, contributing to a clearer understanding of its financial condition. Since EV goes beyond just stock market value to incorporate debt structure and asset liquidity, it serves as a valuable benchmark for investors comparing company values and making strategic decisions.

FHC (Financial Holdings Company)

FHC refers to a company that owns and operates various subsidiaries providing diverse financial services. These companies typically include banks, insurance companies, securities firms, and other financial institutions, leveraging the management and control of these subsidiaries to create synergy and enhance efficiency. Financial holding companies can strengthen the overall group's competitiveness by utilizing the expertise and resources of each subsidiary. FHCs have the advantage of providing integrated financial services that meet a wide range of customer needs while complying with regulatory requirements. This structure enhances risk diversification and capital efficiency, contributing to improved competitiveness in the global market. Additionally, financial holding companies play a crucial role in responding swiftly to changing financial environments and creating new business opportunities.

FI (Financial Investor)

FI refers to individuals or institutions that seek returns by investing in assets. Financial investors allocate their capital across various financial assets such as stocks, bonds, real estate, and derivatives, aiming to maximize capital gains by taking advantage of market volatility. They make investment decisions based on specialized knowledge and analytical skills, setting either short-term or long-term investment objectives. Financial investors typically construct asset portfolios to diversify risk and remain attentive to market changes. These investors can take the form of institutional entities like fund managers, hedge funds, and asset management companies, as well as individual investors. They play a crucial role in supporting economic growth and corporate capital raising, functioning as significant participants in capital markets.

FM (Facility Management)

FM refers to a comprehensive management technique related to the operation, maintenance, safety, and efficient management of buildings and facilities. The primary goal of facility management is to provide a safe and convenient environment for users while maximizing the value and performance of assets. It includes various services such as maintenance of buildings, cleaning, security, energy management, and space planning, playing a crucial role in enhancing operational efficiency within an organization. Facility management contributes to improving employee satisfaction and productivity while promoting cost reduction and resource optimization. An effective FM system seeks sustainable development and environmentally friendly operational practices, as well as compliance with legal requirements. FM has become an essential element across various industries and is increasingly important in the modern complex building operating environment.

FMV (Fair Market Value)

FMV refers to the price at which an asset or property would sell in an open market under normal conditions, where a reasonable buyer is willing to pay. It serves as a standard for valuing assets, based on transactions conducted under non-coercive conditions between sellers and buyers. FMV is commonly used in various situations such as taxation, mergers and acquisitions, financial reporting, and dispute resolution. The fair market value is determined by considering economic conditions, the condition of the asset, market supply and demand, and the transaction prices of similar assets. It can be assessed by professionals or derived from comparable transactions, playing a critical role in identifying the objective value of a specific asset. FMV is an essential concept for ensuring fair and transparent transactions and contributes to a clear understanding of a company's asset value.

FRM (Financial Risk Management)

FRM refers to a strategic approach for identifying, assessing, monitoring, and controlling various financial risks faced by businesses or financial institutions. Financial risks include market risk, credit risk, liquidity risk, and operational risk. FRM focuses on effectively managing these risks to maintain the financial stability and sustainability of an organization. It involves minimizing risks through risk assessment models, hedge strategies, and the establishment of policies and procedures that support the achievement of corporate objectives. By implementing FRM, companies can reduce unexpected losses, enhance capital efficiency, and ensure regulatory compliance. FRM plays a crucial role in all areas of an organization, not just in financial institutions, and requires expertise in risk management and strategic thinking.

FS (Feasibility Study)

FS refers to the analytical process conducted to evaluate the viability of a project or business. It assesses whether the project is feasible from economic, technical, legal, and operational perspectives, providing crucial information for determining the likelihood of the project's success. Key elements include market research, cost analysis, profitability forecasting, and resource evaluation. A feasibility study supports investors and stakeholders in making informed decisions and is essential for demonstrating the project's realizability. By reducing uncertainties and promoting efficient resource allocation, FS is a necessary step before embarking on new business ideas or large-scale projects, laying the groundwork for successful execution.

GCF (Green Climate Fund)

GCF is an international organization established to provide financial support for developing countries to promote low-carbon and climate-resilient development in response to climate change. Founded in 2010 as part of the Paris Agreement, the fund supports projects and programs aimed at adapting to and mitigating climate change worldwide. GCF employs various financing mechanisms to assist national and regional climate response strategies. It plays a crucial role in helping developing countries reduce risks associated with climate change and achieve sustainable development goals. By enhancing climate response capabilities and promoting the development of clean energy technologies and infrastructure, GCF contributes to minimizing the negative impacts of climate change. The fund collaborates with national governments, the private sector, and non-governmental organizations to improve the efficiency of climate financing and contribute to international efforts for sustainable climate change action.

GRI (Global Reporting Initiative)

GRI is an international framework that assists organizations in transparently reporting their economic, environmental, and social impacts. GRI provides guidelines and standards necessary for companies and other organizations to prepare sustainability reports, enabling them to communicate their sustainability performance to various stakeholders and investors. The initiative aims to quantitatively and qualitatively assess non-financial performance, thereby supporting better decision-making processes. By integrating sustainability-related indicators and performance, GRI enhances corporate social responsibility and increases transparency, thereby boosting corporate credibility. Through these efforts, GRI plays a significant role in achieving sustainable development goals and improving the relationship between businesses and society.

GT (Group Technology)

GT is a management and design approach that maximizes efficiency by grouping similar parts or products in the production process. This technology focuses on enhancing production efficiency by utilizing the similarities in product design and manufacturing processes, optimizing inventory management, production planning, and job allocation. GT is commonly used in machining, assembly, and automation systems, where parts with similar shapes and functions are grouped together to reduce inefficiencies in the production process. It contributes to improving productivity and quality while also lowering manufacturing costs. Additionally, GT promotes the use of standardized parts, increasing consistency in part design and production. This approach is utilized across various industries and has become a vital strategy for maximizing efficiency, especially in mass production environments.

HRD (Human Resources Development)

HRD refers to the strategic process of effectively managing and developing an organization's human resources. It includes training and development programs aimed at enhancing employees' skills, knowledge, and competencies, thereby supporting the achievement of organizational goals and strengthening competitiveness. HRD plays a crucial role in fostering continuous learning and growth within the organization, helping employees contribute to the organization's objectives while advancing their own careers. Various training programs, mentoring, career development plans, and performance evaluation systems are employed to facilitate this process. HRD is a vital component of human resource management, contributing to improved organizational performance and employee satisfaction.

HTBC (Historical Trend Base Change)

HTBC refers to a methodology that uses past data and trends to predict future changes or formulate strategies. This approach focuses on analyzing historical patterns and trends to help businesses effectively respond to changes in market conditions, consumer behavior, and financial performance. HTBC provides insights necessary for business decision-making through data analysis and predictive modeling. It plays a crucial role in developing sustainable growth strategies and optimizing risk management and resource allocation. By analyzing past performance and market reactions, organizations can capture future opportunities and prepare for anticipated challenges. This methodology is particularly valuable as a strategic tool for adapting to changing market situations. HTBC enables organizations to make informed decisions that enhance their competitive edge in dynamic environments.

IA (Information Asymmetry)

IA refers to an economic situation that occurs when there is a disparity in the quantity and quality of information between trading parties. This situation arises when one side possesses more information than the other or when there are differences in the interpretation of information, leading to imbalanced conditions in transactions. Information asymmetry is commonly seen in financial markets, insurance, and real estate transactions, potentially resulting in market failures or inefficient decision-making. It creates trust issues between buyers and sellers, which can increase transaction costs and heighten market uncertainty. For example, in the used car market, if the seller conceals information about the vehicle's defects, the buyer may struggle to make an appropriate pricing decision. To mitigate this, methods such as information disclosure, standardized information provision, and third-party certification are employed. Reducing information asymmetry contributes to promoting fair transactions and enhancing market efficiency.

IP (Intellectual Property)

IP refers to the legal rights that protect the ideas, inventions, designs, brands, and other intellectual creations of their creators. It exists in various forms, such as copyrights, patents, trademarks, and industrial designs, granting creators exclusive rights to use their works or inventions for a specified period. This protection allows creators to safeguard the time and resources they have invested, enabling them to realize economic value from their creations. Intellectual property is a crucial element in promoting innovation and creativity, providing a foundation for businesses and individuals to develop and commercialize new ideas. Protecting IP enhances competitiveness, facilitates market differentiation, and defends creations against unauthorized use or infringement. Therefore, IP is considered a significant asset in the modern economy, making effective management and protection essential.

IPO (Initial Public Offering)

IPO refers to the process by which a company first offers its shares to the general public and gets listed on a stock exchange. During this process, the company raises capital and distributes ownership of the company to shareholders. Through an IPO, the company attracts funds from new investors and secures capital for growth and operational expenses. Going public is a significant milestone for a company, enhancing its credibility and transparency while increasing brand value. Additionally, after the IPO, shares can be traded in the market, allowing fluctuations in stock value to reflect the company's financial performance. However, an IPO comes with high regulatory requirements and public obligations, necessitating thorough preparation and strategic planning by the company.

IPR (Intellectual Property Rights)

IPR refers to the legal rights granted to creators for their intellectual creations. These rights exist in various forms, including copyrights, patents, trademarks, and industrial designs, allowing creators to protect their works or inventions. Such rights help creators realize the economic value of their creative efforts and prevent unauthorized use by others. Intellectual property rights are crucial in promoting innovation and creativity, providing a foundation for businesses and individuals to protect and commercialize new ideas. Protecting IP strengthens competitiveness, enables differentiation in the market, and helps prevent legal disputes. Therefore, IPR is considered an essential asset in the modern economy, and effective management and protection of these rights are vital.

IR (Investor Relations)

IR refers to the activities involved in communication and relationship management between a company and its investors. The primary purpose of IR is to provide investors with information about the company's business model, financial performance, strategies, and market environment, thereby building trust and supporting investment decisions. This approach enhances transparency and helps maintain positive relationships with shareholders and potential investors. Investor relations activities include regular financial reports, annual shareholder meetings, investor presentations, and media communications. Through IR, companies deliver information that aligns with market expectations and share strategic directions aimed at maximizing corporate value. An effective IR strategy contributes to building trust with investors and stabilizing the company's market value.

ISDS (Investor-State Dispute Settlement)

ISDS refers to a mechanism for resolving legal disputes that may arise in international investment between an investor and the host state. This mechanism is primarily used when multinational corporations have grievances regarding contracts or investments with foreign governments, providing a pathway for investors to take legal action against the state. ISDS plays a crucial role in protecting investors' rights and enhancing confidence in foreign investment. It allows investors to seek resolution from a neutral third party when they believe they have been unfairly harmed by the state's legal or administrative actions. However, ISDS has faced criticism for potentially infringing on state sovereignty and imposing limitations on public policy.

KMS (Knowledge Management System)

KMS refers to an IT-based system that helps organizations efficiently collect, store, share, and utilize knowledge and information. It centralizes employees' experiences, expertise, processes, and documents, enhancing accessibility and usability while managing the organization's knowledge assets. Knowledge management systems contribute to improving decision-making processes, fostering innovation, and increasing operational efficiency. By enabling employees to quickly find and share the information they need, KMS reduces repetitive tasks and supports the growth of a learning organization. It has become an essential tool for strengthening a company's competitiveness and supporting sustainable development.

KPI (Key Performance Indicator)

KPI refers to important performance metrics established to measure and evaluate an organization's achievement of its goals. It helps assess specific objectives and performance based on data aligned with the company's strategic direction. KPIs can be categorized into financial indicators (e.g., revenue growth rate, net profit) and non-financial indicators (e.g., customer satisfaction, employee turnover rate). They play a crucial role in monitoring organizational performance and making necessary adjustments to achieve targets. Effective KPIs should be measurable, clear, and capable of reflecting changes over time. They serve as foundational data for executives and teams to strive for goal achievement and develop strategies for performance improvement.

M&A (Mergers & Acquisition)

M&A refers to the process by which a company acquires another company or two companies merge to form a new entity. An acquisition involves one company purchasing the shares of another company to secure ownership, while a merger refers to the integration of two or more companies on equal terms to create a new corporation. M&A serves as a crucial strategy for corporate growth, contributing to market share expansion, technology acquisition, cost reduction, and synergy creation. This process requires thorough due diligence and assessment, involving complex legal, financial, and operational procedures. M&A plays a significant role in enhancing a company's competitiveness and entering new markets, and when executed successfully, it can increase the long-term growth and sustainability of the company.

M&O (Monopoly and Oligopoly)

M&O refers to two forms of market structure, distinguished by the number of suppliers in the market and how prices are determined. Monopoly is a situation where a single company exclusively supplies a product or service in the market. In this case, the monopolist can freely set prices, and there are high barriers to market entry, resulting in little to no competition. While monopolies can lead to limited consumer choice and higher prices, they may also yield cost savings due to large-scale production. Oligopoly describes a market structure where a small number of companies dominate. These firms influence each other's pricing and production decisions. In an oligopoly, companies compete, but price reductions or changes in production levels can provoke responses from rivals. This market often sees high brand loyalty and significant product differentiation, and there is potential for collaboration among firms.

MBA (Master of Business Administration)

MBA is a graduate program aimed at enhancing expertise in management and business-related fields. Typically, MBA courses encompass a wide range of subjects, including management, finance, marketing, human resources, and strategy, designed to equip students with both theoretical knowledge and practical skills essential for operating and managing businesses. The program focuses on preparing individuals for managerial and leadership roles while providing networking opportunities and practical experiences to help graduates succeed in real business environments. Many MBA programs are offered in full-time, part-time, and online formats, contributing to a deeper understanding of entrepreneurship, innovation, and global business. The MBA is a popular choice for those seeking career transitions, job advancements, and network expansion.

MBO (Management by Objectives)

MBO is a management technique that involves setting organizational goals and managing performance through specific planning and evaluation aimed at achieving those goals. This process involves collaboration between management and employees to establish goals, evaluate individual and team performance based on these goals, and provide feedback. MBO contributes to enhancing organizational efficiency and motivating employees by clarifying objectives and distributing responsibilities. The technique focuses on aligning goals with the organization's strategic direction and developing performance indicators for achieving those goals. MBO promotes continuous growth and improvement through performance measurement, feedback provision, and the establishment of action plans for performance enhancement. This approach is useful for aligning individual and organizational goals and has become an essential tool for overall performance improvement.

MS (Market Share)

MS is the percentage of a specific company's sales or revenue in relation to the total market, indicating the proportion of the market that the company occupies. Typically expressed as a percentage, market share serves as a crucial measure for evaluating a company's competitiveness and position within the market. A high market share generally signifies that the company holds a strong position in the market, which can help enhance brand recognition among consumers. Market share is utilized for performance analysis, strategy formulation, and comparisons with competitors, allowing companies to identify growth opportunities and gather information necessary for product or service improvements. Understanding market share is essential for assessing how successfully a company competes in the market, and it contributes to the development of effective marketing and sales strategies by management.

NBD (New Business Development)

NBD refers to the process by which a company explores and develops new market, product, or service opportunities to enhance growth and profitability. This strategic approach aims to create new revenue streams beyond existing business areas and includes activities such as market research, idea generation, product development, and marketing strategy formulation. New business development is essential for companies to adapt to changing market environments and maintain competitiveness. Through NBD, companies can meet customer needs and provide innovative solutions, thereby expanding their market share. It often serves as a core element of a company's sustainable growth strategy, allowing management to establish a direction to realize long-term vision and increase corporate value.

O&M (Operation & Maintenance)

O&M refers to the process of managing the efficient operation and continuous maintenance of facilities, systems, or equipment. This process focuses on ensuring that assets maintain optimal performance while preventing failures or emergencies. O&M is commonly applied across various industries, particularly in energy, public infrastructure, manufacturing, and transportation systems. It encompasses regular inspections, repairs, software updates, and performance monitoring to manage the asset lifecycle. Through effective O&M, companies can reduce operational costs, enhance efficiency, and strengthen safety. Proper execution of O&M increases asset uptime and improves overall operational efficiency, thereby enhancing the company's competitiveness. Additionally, data analysis collected during the O&M process enables continuous optimization of asset performance and helps develop future maintenance plans, leading to long-term cost savings. This management system has become essential for companies aiming to achieve sustainable growth in competitive markets.

OBS (Organizational Breakdown Structure)

OBS is a structural tool used in project management to clearly define and visually represent the roles and responsibilities of the project team within the organization. It illustrates the hierarchical structure of personnel and resources associated with each component of the project, helping to clarify each team member's responsibilities and authority. OBS facilitates project management and coordination, contributing to more efficient resource allocation and communication. This allows project managers to promote collaboration among team members and effectively coordinate roles to achieve project goals. The organizational breakdown structure plays a crucial role in managing project complexity and maximizing team performance.

OC (Opportunity Cost)

OC refers to the value of the alternatives that are forgone when a particular choice is made. It is an important concept in economics used to measure the benefits of alternatives that are not utilized when resources are allocated to a single use. In other words, the value of the alternative that is not obtained due to a decision becomes the opportunity cost. Opportunity cost is essential for efficient resource allocation and decision-making, as every choice comes with alternatives that must be considered. For example, if an investor decides to invest in Asset A, the returns from that asset may be lower than the returns from investing in Asset B; in this case, the returns from Asset B represent the opportunity cost. By considering opportunity costs, individuals and organizations can make better choices and utilize resources effectively. This analysis applies widely, from personal consumption decisions to strategic corporate investments, contributing to the maximization of long-term benefits. Therefore, a clear understanding of opportunity cost is crucial for making rational decisions.

OMO (Open Market Operation)

OMO refers to the monetary policy tool used by central banks to regulate money supply and interest rates through the buying and selling of financial assets such as government bonds in the market. This operation is primarily employed to manage liquidity in the economy and prevent inflation or deflation. When the central bank purchases assets, liquidity in the market increases, and conversely, selling assets reduces liquidity, which can raise interest rates. This action plays a crucial role in maintaining financial market stability and promoting economic growth. For example, during an economic recession, the central bank may buy assets to increase liquidity and lower borrowing costs for businesses and households, thereby encouraging consumption and investment. Conversely, in situations where inflation is a concern, the central bank may sell assets to decrease the money supply and raise interest rates.

OR (Operational Risk)

OR refers to the risk of loss that can arise from a company's everyday operational processes, encompassing all risks associated with people, processes, systems, and external events. This type of risk can arise from various factors, including employee mistakes, system failures, process breakdowns, fraud, and natural disasters. These risks can negatively impact not only a company's financial performance but also its reputation. Managing operational risk focuses on identifying, assessing, monitoring, and controlling these risks to ensure organizational stability and sustainability. Effective operational risk management contributes to improving business processes, optimizing financial performance, and complying with legal and regulatory requirements. Therefore, operational risk has become a crucial management aspect across all industries, requiring continuous monitoring and improvement.

PAM (Plant Asset Management)

PAM refers to the systems and strategies used to efficiently manage and operate assets within industrial facilities. This management system focuses on maintaining optimized performance throughout the asset lifecycle, reducing maintenance costs, and maximizing uptime. PAM is particularly important in industries such as manufacturing, energy, chemicals, and other heavy industries. Asset management involves regular inspections, preventive maintenance, and asset performance analysis to maximize asset value and improve operational efficiency.

PF (Project Financing)

PF refers to a financial structure used to raise funds necessary for carrying out a specific project, typically securing financing based on the project's profitability and assets. This approach is commonly employed in capital-intensive ventures such as large-scale infrastructure projects, energy development, and construction. Project financing usually involves collaboration with various stakeholders, including lenders, investors, and government agencies. A key feature of project financing is that funding is based on the cash flow generated by the project itself, meaning that loan repayments come from the revenues generated once the project is operational. This structure allows participating companies to reduce capital burdens and distribute risks, as it does not rely on the general assets of the company. Overall, project financing provides a critical financial foundation for the successful execution of specific projects and is regarded as an important means of supporting sustainable development and economic growth.

PFV (Project Financing Vehicle)

PFV refers to a legal structure or entity designed to raise project financing funds for a specific project. It plays a role in securing funding based on the project's assets and revenues while managing relationships with funders, investors, and creditors. This mechanism is commonly used in large-scale infrastructure projects, energy development, and construction projects. PFV contributes to optimizing the financial structure of the project, distributing risk, and providing a stable revenue source for investors and creditors. Typically, a PFV is established as an independent legal entity that manages the cash flows generated by the project and executes contracts related to the project.

R&D (Research and Development)

R&D refers to the systematic activities conducted by companies or organizations to develop new products, services, or technologies, or to improve existing ones. In the research phase, innovative ideas and technologies based on basic or applied sciences are explored, while the development phase involves practicalizing these ideas and implementing them as actual products or services. R&D is essential for maintaining a company's competitiveness and strengthening its market position. Through R&D, companies can foster innovation and provide products that meet customer needs, thereby expanding their market share. Additionally, R&D is considered a key component of long-term growth strategies and an important investment for sustainable development. Successful R&D activities can enhance a company's profitability and secure a technological edge.

SI (Strategic Investor)

SI refers to individuals or institutions that invest in specific companies to support growth or achieve strategic objectives. Unlike purely financial investors, strategic investors focus on maximizing synergies and establishing long-term relationships by leveraging the operations, technology, or market access of the companies they invest in. They can share resources or build cooperative relationships to enhance competitiveness within the industry. Strategic investors support their targets through M&A (mergers and acquisitions), capital investments, or partnerships, contributing to the growth of the invested companies and creating new market opportunities. This investment approach can benefit both parties and plays a crucial role in accelerating innovation and technological development within the companies involved.

SOW (Share of Wallet)

SOW refers to the proportion of a specific customer's spending that is allocated to a particular company, indicating the portion of the customer's overall expenditure that the company captures. This concept serves as a vital metric for evaluating how much revenue a business generates from its existing customers. SOW helps businesses understand customers' spending patterns and analyze the factors influencing their purchasing decisions. Increasing SOW is part of strategies aimed at enhancing customer loyalty and maximizing the value of existing customers, making it a key objective of marketing and sales strategies. By meeting customers' needs and preferences, companies can increase SOW, thereby promoting revenue growth and enhancing competitiveness.

SPC (Special Purpose Company)

SPC refers to a legal entity established for the purpose of executing specific projects or transactions, typically used to manage risks by segregating assets, liabilities, and legal responsibilities. SPCs are primarily utilized in real estate development, financial transactions, and investment projects, providing a structure that allows for independent management of asset ownership or specific business activities. They help in distributing asset risks and offering stability to investors or creditors. For example, by assigning the assets and liabilities of a specific project to an SPC, the project's performance can be assessed separately from the original company's financial status. This structure is frequently employed in projects requiring substantial capital investment and can also contribute to regulatory compliance and tax planning.

SPM (Strategic Performance Measurement)

SPM refers to the systems and processes used to evaluate and manage performance in order to achieve an organization's goals and strategies. It encompasses not only financial indicators but also non-financial metrics, providing a comprehensive analysis of the extent to which strategic objectives are met. This system employs various tools, such as KPI (Key Performance Indicator) and BSC (Balanced Score Card), to measure performance and suggest areas for improvement. Strategic performance measurement establishes performance criteria that align with the organization's long-term objectives, thereby providing useful information for decision-making processes. This enables management to analyze the current performance of the organization and, if necessary, adjust strategies or reallocate resources.

SRI (Socially Responsible Investment)

SRI refers to an approach to investment decision-making that considers not only a company's financial performance but also its environmental, social responsibility, and ethical standards. SRI investors evaluate whether a company's operations have a positive social impact, selecting investment targets based on various criteria such as human rights, environmental protection, labor conditions, and corporate governance. Socially responsible investment reflects the intention of investors to achieve social value while pursuing financial gains, which can contribute to the sustainability and long-term growth of companies. SRI is closely linked to ESG (Environmental, Social, and Governance) investing, and as environmental and social issues become increasingly important, many investors and institutions are adopting the principles of SRI.

SWOT (Strengths, Weaknesses, Opportunities, Threats)

SWOT is a tool used to support strategic decision-making by evaluating an organization's internal strengths and weaknesses, as well as external opportunities and threats. This analytical method is applied in various fields such as business strategy development, marketing planning, and competitive analysis, playing a crucial role in assessing the current state of an organization and setting future directions.

1) Strengths: These are the areas where the organization excels, providing a competitive advantage. Examples include brand recognition, technological capabilities, and customer loyalty.
2) Weaknesses: These are aspects of the organization that require improvement and could lead to a decrease in competitiveness. For instance, low quality, financial difficulties, and workforce shortages may fall under this category.
3) Opportunities: These are external factors that can positively influence the organization, including market growth potential or emerging trends. Examples consist of entering new markets or technological innovations.
4) Threats: These are external factors that may negatively impact the organization, such as increased competition or tighter regulations. Examples include economic downturns and the growth of competitors.

TCO (Total Cost of Ownership)

TCO is a concept that evaluates the total cost of owning an asset, including not only the purchase price but also all costs associated with operation, maintenance, support, and disposal. TCO enables a more realistic financial analysis by considering both initial purchase costs and long-term expenses. Conducting a TCO analysis plays a crucial role for businesses in understanding the costs throughout the entire lifecycle of an asset and making cost-effective decisions. For instance, in the case of IT equipment or software, it is essential to consider not just the purchase price, but also installation costs, maintenance costs, training expenses, and energy costs.

VOC (Voice of Customer)

VOC is a concept that involves collecting and analyzing customer needs, expectations, preferences, and experiences to enable businesses to improve their products and services with a customercentric approach. By gathering customer feedback, VOC plays a crucial role in enhancing product or service quality and increasing customer satisfaction. Information is collected through various methods, including surveys, interviews, feedback forms, social media, and reviews. By analyzing this data, businesses can understand customer opinions and incorporate them into product development or service improvements, thereby meeting customer demands and strengthening their competitive edge.

Part 3 International Trade

AAP (Age Additional Premium) 227

AB (Accepting Bank) 227

AB (Advising Bank) 227

AC (Account Current) 228

ACC (Air Cargo Consolidator) 228

ACT (Air Cargo Transportation) 229

ADR (European Agreement concerning the International Carriage of Dangerous Goods by Road) 229

AIV (Agreed Insurable Value) 230

ALB (America Land Bridge) 230

ALC (Acceptance Letter of Credit) 231

AMR (Agreed Minimum Rate) 231

AMS (Automatic Manifest System Charge) 231

AOG (Arrival of Goods) 232

AON (Accident of Navigation) 232

AR (Advance Remittance) 232

AR (Acceptance Rate) 233

AS (Annual Survey) 233

ASR (Airport Surveillance Radar) 234

ASRS (Automated Storage and Retrieval System)	234
ATA (Actual Time of Arrival)	234
ATD (Actual Time of Departure)	235
ATL (Absolute Total Loss)	235
AWB (Air-way Bill)	236
BA (Banker's Acceptance)	236
BAF (Bunker Adjustment Factor)	236
BL (Bill of Lading)	237
CA (Correction Advice)	237
CAD (Cash against Documents)	237
CAF (Currency Adjustment Factor)	238
CBM (Cubic Meter)	238
CBR (Critical Bunker Recovery)	238
CCF (Collect Charge Fee)	239
CCF (Container Cleaning Fee)	239
CFR (Cost and Freight)	239
CFS (Container Freight Station)	240
CGT (Compensated Gross Tonnage)	240

CI (Commercial Invoice)	241
CIF (Cost Insurance and Freight)	241
CLC (Confirmed Letter of Credit)	241
CO (Certificate of Origin)	242
COD (Cash on Delivery)	242
CONSOL (Consolidation)	242
CP (Charter Party)	243
CPFR (Collaborative Planning Forecasting Replenishment)	243
CPT (Carriage Paid To)	243
CT (Container Terminal)	244
CW (Chargeable Weight)	244
CY (Container Yard)	244
DC (Demurrage Charge)	245
DC (Detention Charge)	245
DC (Drayage Charge)	245
DD (Demand Draft)	245
DDC (Destination Delivery Charge)	246
DDP (Delivered Duty Paid)	246

DDU (Delivered Duty Unpaid)	246
DEQ (Delivered Ex Quay)	247
DES (Delivered Ex Ship)	247
DGR (Dangerous Goods Regulations)	247
DLC (Documentary Letter of Credit)	247
DO (Delivery Order)	248
DP (Document against Payment)	248
DS (Docking Survey)	249
DWT (Dead Weight Tonnage)	249
EBS (Emergency Bunker Surcharge)	249
ECA (Export Credit Agency)	250
EL (Export License)	250
EOC (Error and Omission Clause)	250
ETA (Estimated Time of Arrival)	250
ETD (Estimated Time of Departure)	251
EXW (Ex-Work)	251
FAF (Fuel Adjustment Factor)	251
FAS (Free Alongside Ship)	252

FC (Forwarding Company)	252
FCA (Free Carrier)	252
FCL (Full Container Load)	252
FEU (Forty-foot Equivalent Units)	253
FIATA (International Federation of Freight Forwarders Associations)	253
FIFO (First In First Out)	253
FL (Freight List)	254
FO (Firm Offer)	254
FOB (Free On Board)	254
FSC (Fuel Surcharge)	254
FT (Free Time)	255
FTA (Free Trade Agreement)	255
GA (General Average)	255
GATT (General Agreement on Tariffs and Trade)	256
GCA (Ground Controlled Approach)	256
GL (Germanischer Lloyd)	256
GPI (Ground Position Indicator)	256
GPWS (Ground Proximity Warning System)	257

GRI (General Rate Increase)	257
GT (Gross Tonnage)	257
H&M (Hull & Machinery Insurance)	258
HC (Handling Charge)	258
IACS (International Association of Classification Societies)	258
IC (Inspection Certificate)	258
ICD (Inland Container Depot)	259
ID (Import Declaration)	259
IL (Import License)	259
ILC (Irrevocable Letter of Credit)	259
ILS (Instrument Landing System)	260
IMDG (International Maritime Dangerous Goods)	260
IMO (International Maritime Organization)	260
INCOTERMS (International Rules for the Interpretation of Trade Terms)	260
IP (Insurance Policy)	261
IPI (Interior Point Intermodal)	261
IS (Intermediate Survey)	261
KIFFA (Korea International Freight Forwarders Association)	262

LC (Letter of Credit)	262
LCL (Less than Container Load)	262
LG (Letter of Guarantee)	263
LI (Letter of Indemnity)	263
LTA (Long Term Agreement)	263
MBL (Master Bill of Landing)	263
MCI (Marine Cargo Insurance)	264
MF (Manifest)	264
MFCS (Manifest Consolidation System)	264
MLB (Mini Land Bridge)	264
MLC (Master Letter of Credit)	265
MR (Mate's Receipt)	265
MT (Metric Ton)	265
MTO (Multimodal Transport Operator)	265
MV (Mother Vessel)	266
NLC (Negotiation Letter of Credit)	266
NVOCC (Non Vessel Operating Common Carrier)	266
OA (Open Account)	266

OBL (Original Bill of Lading)	267
ODM (Original Development/Design Manufacturing)	267
OEM (Original Equipment Manufacturing)	267
OF (Ocean Freight)	268
OSC (Over Storage Charge)	268
OTC (Open Top Container)	268
PA (Particular Average)	268
PCS (Port Congestion Surcharge)	269
PL (Packing List)	269
PSS (Peak Season Surcharge)	269
RIPI (Revised Interior Point Intermodal)	269
RORO (Roll On Roll Off Vessel)	270
RT (Revenue Ton)	270
RVP (Reid Vapor Pressure)	270
RVR (Runway Visual Range)	270
RVV (Runway Visibility Value)	271
SBL (Surrender Bill of Lading)	271
SBL (Switch Bill of Lading)	271

SC (Service Contract)	271
SC (Shipping Company)	272
SC (Shoring Charge)	272
SCR (Specific Commodity Rate)	272
SD (Shipping Date)	272
SD (Shipping Document)	273
SGS (Societe Generale de Surveillance)	273
SO (Sipping Order)	273
SOC (Shipper's Own Container)	273
SR (Shipping Request)	274
SSC (Security Surcharge)	274
TC (Tally Charge)	274
TC (Time Charter)	274
TC (Trucking Charge)	275
TEU (Twenty Foot Equivalent Unit)	275
THC (Terminal Handling Charge)	275
TL (Total Loss)	275
TR (Trust Receipt)	275

TS (Trans-shipment)	276
TSCS (Trans-Siberian Container Service)	276
TSR (Trans-Siberian Railway)	276
TT (Telegraphic Transfer)	276
TT (Transit Time)	277
TTC (Through Transport Club)	277
TVP (True Vapor Pressure)	277
TWRA (Transpacific Westbound Rate Agreement)	277
UCP (Uniform Customs and Practice for Documentary Credits)	277
ULC (Usance Letter of Credit)	278
VOY (Voyage)	278
VSL (Vessel)	278
WA (With Average)	278
WCS (Weight Surcharge)	279
WFG (Wharfage)	279
WRS (War Risk Surcharge)	279
WT (Weight Ton)	279

AAP (Age Additional Premium)

AAP is an additional cost imposed on cargo transportation insurance premiums based on the age of the vessel calculated from the date of its launch. The age of the vessel is an important factor in determining the insurance premium. Generally, the insurance premium for loaded vessels is determined according to the standards of classification and age, but vessels older than 15 years (excluding regular vessels) are excluded from these conditions. For vessels over 15 years old, the likelihood of mechanical failure or accidents increases, prompting insurers to collect additional premiums under the name of age additional premium to reflect the additional risk. This AAP plays a critical role in enhancing the safety of maritime transport and managing the financial risks for insurers.

AB (Accepting Bank)

AB is the bank that receives a request from the exporter's bank in a letter of credit transaction, approves the terms of the letter of credit, and facilitates the exporter's receipt of payment. It assumes the obligation to pay for the goods or services provided by the exporter and generally enhances the reliability of the exporter's transactions. The accepting bank ensures the safety of the transaction through the letter of credit and assists the exporter in receiving payment from the importer. Additionally, it reviews the documents requested by the exporter to ensure they comply with the conditions of the letter of credit and manages the process of payment after approval.

AB (Advising Bank)

AB is the bank that notifies the exporter of the letter of credit received from the importer and verifies the conditions specified in the letter of credit. Typically located in the exporter's home country or the trading country, it plays a crucial role in enhancing the safety and reliability of the letter of credit transaction. The advising bank reviews the appropriateness of the letter of credit's contents and confirms the documents and conditions required by the exporter before communicating them to the exporter. Additionally, it may provide advice on the letter of credit terms to the exporter and assist in understanding the document submission and payment procedures.

AC (Account Current)

AC refers to an accounting ledger that records transaction details between parties, settling mutual debts and credits. It is primarily used in business transactions between companies and includes details of payments, credits, and debits for each transaction. The account current allows for a comprehensive view of all transaction records over a specific period, facilitating the settlement process. It is particularly useful in export-import or trade transactions, helping both parties clarify their current debt and credit status and making settlements easier when they engage in frequent transactions. This enables companies to manage their finances efficiently and enhances transparency in transactions, thereby strengthening trust.

ACC (Air Cargo Consolidator)

ACC refers to a service provider that combines multiple small shipments into a single larger shipment for transportation by airlines. These consolidators gather various customers' cargo to reduce shipping costs and improve transport efficiency by collaborating with airlines. ACCs offer lower transportation costs compared to individual shipments and handle all necessary procedures to safely collect and deliver customers' goods to their destinations. They also provide a range of services, including logistics management, customs procedures, and transport scheduling, to facilitate more convenient shipping for customers. This role is particularly important in international logistics, allowing customers greater flexibility in shipping small cargo and enabling quick responses to market changes. ACCs are vital partners in maximizing the efficiency of air cargo transport and supporting customers in reducing logistics costs.

ACT (Air Cargo Transportation)

ACT refers to the service of transporting goods using aircraft. This mode of transportation is suitable for products that require quick delivery or for moving large quantities internationally. It typically responds to urgent product demands and has the advantage of reaching destinations in a shorter time compared to other transportation methods. Air cargo transportation operates through a fast, safe, and globally connected network, handling a variety of items, including food, pharmaceuticals, and electronic devices. It is conducted in collaboration with airlines, freight forwarders, and logistics companies, playing a crucial role in export and import transactions. Additionally, air cargo transportation enhances customer satisfaction through expedited customs procedures and efficient logistics management.

ADR (European Agreement concerning the International Carriage of Dangerous Goods by Road)

ADR is a European agreement that establishes regulations for the international transportation of dangerous goods by road. This agreement was created to ensure the safe transportation of hazardous materials and to minimize accidents and environmental damage that may occur during road transport. ADR provides consistent standards for the transportation of dangerous goods across Europe, helping transport operators and relevant parties comply with legal requirements. It defines hazardous materials and specifies requirements for packaging, labeling, transport documentation, training, and vehicle specifications to create a safe transportation.

AIV (Agreed Insurable Value)

AIV is the value of an asset that is mutually agreed upon by the insured and the insurer in an insurance contract. This value represents the amount both parties agree upon when the insured takes out a policy, serving as the basis for claims payments. AIV is commonly used in marine and cargo insurance and plays a critical role in evaluating the value of goods, machinery, and equipment. When the insured purchases coverage, the insurer uses this value to determine the premium and decide on the amount to be paid in case of a loss. AIV helps reduce disputes during the claims assessment process and ensures that the insured reflects the actual value of the asset when paying a fair premium. This contributes to guaranteeing the safety of cargo in international trade and providing a stable financial foundation for asset protection.

ALB (America Land Bridge)

ALB is a logistics route developed by Sea Train in 1972, which involves transporting goods from the Far East to the U.S. West Coast by sea, followed by land transportation across the continent via rail, and finally shipping back by sea to Atlantic coastal ports in the eastern United States. This system connects Siberia with the North American continent, allowing cargo to be shipped from Far Eastern ports to Pacific Coast ports (such as LA and Seattle) and then transported overland to Atlantic ports (such as New York, Baltimore, and Miami) en route to Europe. It offers significant freight cost savings and reduced transit times compared to traditional all-sea shipping and the Trans-Siberian Railway. This route effectively serves as a "land bridge" connecting the long distances across the U.S. continent, contributing to enhanced logistics efficiency between Asia and Europe through the U.S. ALB facilitates smoother and more cost-effective trade flows between major global markets.

ALC (Acceptance Letter of Credit)

ALC is a type of letter of credit issued by the importer to the exporter, which specifies the documents and conditions necessary for the exporter to receive payment after the shipment of goods. When the exporter submits the designated documents, the financial institution provides a promise to pay, serving as an important means of ensuring trust in international trade. The acceptance letter of credit plays a crucial role in ensuring the safe delivery of cargo and the smooth progress of transactions. Through the ALC, exporters can secure payment for the shipped goods, while importers can confirm the safe arrival of the cargo before making the promised payment. This enhances transparency in transactions and helps build trust between both parties.

AMR (Agreed Minimum Rate)

AMR is a system that establishes a minimum rate agreed upon between the transportation service provider and the customer, ensuring that transportation costs do not fall below a certain level under specific conditions. This helps transportation providers maintain economic stability and offers customers consistent pricing, thereby contributing to the quality of service. The agreed minimum rate plays a crucial role, especially in international trade and maritime transport, enhancing the transparency of contracts and strengthening trust between both parties. This system supports sustainable operations for transportation providers while allowing customers to access services at predictable costs.

AMS (Automatic Manifest System Charge)

AMS is a system required by the U.S. Customs and Border Protection (CBP) for customs declaration of maritime and air cargo. This system automatically collects and manages manifest information for exported and imported goods, helping customs authorities verify the safety and legality of the cargo. AMS enables accurate and swift customs processing, contributing to the efficiency of the logistics system. This facilitates the smooth flow of cargo and identifies potential risks in advance, thereby enhancing the reliability of trade transactions.

AOG (Arrival of Goods)
AOG refers to the point at which the commencement of a discount or payment deadline is based on the arrival of goods. This term plays a crucial role in international trade, as the moment the goods arrive at their destination serves as the benchmark for determining the start of discount conditions or payment deadlines. AOG contributes to clarifying the terms of transactions through logistics and financial management, supporting the fulfillment of contracts between sellers and buyers. This enhances the transparency of transactions and plays an important role in aligning the expectations of both parties.

AON (Accident of Navigation)
AON refers to accidents that occur during a vessel's voyage and is considered a significant risk factor in maritime transportation. Such incidents can lead to cargo loss, vessel damage, and personal injury, making them important considerations in international trade and marine insurance. Maritime accidents can arise from various causes, including weather conditions, mechanical failures, and human errors, which subsequently affect the insurance company's loss assessment and compensation processes.

AR (Advance Remittance)
AR refers to the method of remitting payment in advance before the delivery of goods or services, commonly used in international trade. This approach enhances the security of transactions by allowing the

seller to receive payment upfront, thereby preventing accounts receivable issues. Advance remittance is particularly prevalent in transactions with unreliable trading partners, serving as a useful strategy to minimize risks associated with the trade.

AR (Acceptance Rate)

AR refers to the ratio of promissory notes presented by the importer that are accepted by the exporter, serving as an important indicator for assessing the reliability of trade transactions. This ratio represents the proportion of accepted notes over a specific period, allowing exporters to secure stable revenues through a high acceptance rate. The acceptance rate can vary based on factors such as creditworthiness, the reliability of trading partners, and market conditions, influenced by the terms of trade contracts or payment methods. For example, if the importer is a trustworthy trading partner, the acceptance rate tends to be higher. AR contributes to enhancing the safety and reliability of payments in international transactions and strengthens the relationships between trade partners.

AS (Annual Survey)

AS refers to the annual inspections conducted to verify that ships, structures, or other marine facilities meet safety and legal requirements. This inspection is a crucial procedure aimed at ensuring operational efficiency and preventing accidents, carried out in accordance with the regulations set forth by the International Maritime Organization (IMO) and related standards. The annual survey evaluates the vessel's mechanical and electrical systems, safety equipment, and structural integrity, and upon completion, a certificate of compliance is issued. These inspections help ship owners meet legal requirements and contribute to the safety of maritime transportation. Additionally, the annual survey plays an important role in determining insurance premiums and securing reliability in international trade.

ASR (Airport Surveillance Radar)

ASR is a radar system used to monitor and track aircraft in the vicinity of an airport. This system provides real-time information on the position and altitude of aircraft, assisting airport air traffic controllers in safely managing and controlling aircraft. ASR is particularly important for accurately identifying the position of aircraft during takeoff and landing phases. The airport surveillance radar plays a crucial role in reducing traffic congestion, enhancing flight safety, and improving operational efficiency at airports. The ASR system can accurately track aircraft even in adverse weather conditions or low visibility, making it essential for ensuring safe flight paths within the airport.

ASRS (Automated Storage and Retrieval System)

ASRS is a technological system designed for the automatic storage and retrieval of goods or materials within a warehouse. This system typically utilizes robots, conveyor systems, and computer software to provide efficient inventory management while optimizing warehouse space and reducing operational costs. ASRS contributes to increased inventory accuracy, reduced human errors, and shorter access times for items. It is becoming increasingly important in logistics and supply chain management, widely used by manufacturers and distributors due to its ability to process large quantities of goods quickly and efficiently.

ATA (Actual Time of Arrival)

ATA is a term used to record the actual arrival time of a flight or cargo, which plays a crucial role in logistics and transportation management.

It is necessary for evaluating transportation efficiency by comparing it to the Estimated Time of Arrival (ETA) and providing accurate information to customers. The actual arrival time is useful for analyzing the causes of delays in transport routes and operational efficiency, allowing logistics managers to improve future transportation planning. ATA has become an essential factor in managing delivery schedules and enhancing customer service in international trade.

ATD (Actual Time of Departure)

ATD is a term used to record the actual departure time of a flight or cargo, playing a crucial role in transportation management and logistics operations. ATD is necessary for evaluating the accuracy and efficiency of transport by comparing it to the Estimated Time of Departure (ETD) and providing reliable information to customers. The actual departure time is useful for analyzing the causes of delays in transport routes and operational efficiency, allowing logistics managers to improve future transportation planning.

ATL (Absolute Total Loss)

ATL refers to a condition in insurance and shipping where cargo or assets are completely destroyed or lost, making recovery impossible. In this scenario, the insured can claim the full amount of the asset under their insurance policy, based on the terms outlined in the contract. Absolute total loss can result from various incidents such as maritime accidents, fires, or theft, and it is a critical factor in risk management within logistics and international trade. In the context of car insurance, ATL plays a key role in loss assessment and claims processes, enabling insurers to handle losses promptly and fairly. Understanding ATL is essential for both insurers and policyholders to ensure effective risk management and claims resolution.

AWB (Air-way Bill)

AWB is a document used in air freight transportation that serves to record the contract and details of the cargo shipment. This document includes information such as the sender, recipient, cargo specifics, and transport route, functioning as a contract proof between the airline and the freight forwarder. The air waybill plays a crucial role in tracking and managing goods, facilitating customs clearance procedures, and handling insurance claims, thus supporting smooth logistics operations in international trade.

BA (Banker's Acceptance)

BA is a financial document used in export-import transactions, where a bank promises to pay a specified amount, guaranteeing payment to the payee. This acceptance typically occurs after the exporter has shipped the goods, and before the importer makes the payment. By endorsing the acceptance, the bank enhances the reliability of the transaction. Banker's acceptances serve as a payment guarantee in trade transactions, allowing exporters to discount the acceptance with financial institutions to obtain immediate funding.

BAF (Bunker Adjustment Factor)

BAF is a surcharge applied in maritime transportation to cover additional costs resulting from fluctuations in fuel prices. This charge is implemented by shipping companies to compensate for increased transportation costs due to rising fuel prices and is specified as part of the transportation contract. The bunker adjustment factor becomes essential, especially during spikes in fuel prices, as it helps shipping lines maintain stable freight costs. BAF is included in the total shipping cost and billed to customers, playing a critical role in establishing predictable transportation costs in international trade. BAF ensures that shipping companies can manage operational costs effectively while providing transparency to customers regarding fuel-related charges.

BL (Bill of Lading)

BL is a document that serves as evidence of the contract between the shipper and the carrier during the transportation of goods, including details of the cargo's ownership, transportation conditions, and recipient information. This document plays a crucial role in maritime shipping and is issued once the shipper has loaded the cargo. The bill of lading acts as significant proof of the transfer of ownership of the goods, allowing the recipient to claim the cargo by presenting this document. Additionally, the BL is important in customs clearance and insurance claims in international trade, contributing to transparency and reliability in logistics management.

CA (Correction Advice)

CA is an official notification sent to correct errors that have occurred in transactions or documents. This document is primarily used when there is a need to amend or rectify the contents of financial transactions, contracts, invoices, and similar documents, playing a crucial role in correcting inaccurate information. The correction advice clearly outlines the amended details and is communicated to the relevant parties, contributing to the accuracy and transparency of transactions. CA is especially essential in international trade, where the accuracy of documents is critical for enhancing trust among related parties or institutions.

CAD (Cash against Documents)

CAD refers to a payment method where the exporter ships the goods and the importer pays for them after submitting the relevant shipping documents. In this system, the exporter forwards the transportation documents to the importer through a bank, and the importer must pay the amount due to receive these documents. Cash against documents is commonly used between reliable trading partners, as it ensures the exporter secures payment while allowing the importer to obtain the necessary documents for customs clearance before the goods arrive.

CAF (Currency Adjustment Factor)

CAF refers to an additional charge applied in maritime or air transportation to reflect changes in costs due to exchange rate fluctuations. This surcharge is primarily used in international trade and is implemented to adjust for the impact of currency value changes on transportation costs. The currency adjustment factor functions as a mechanism to manage risks associated with trading in specific currencies and to ensure the profitability of contracts. This enables carriers to minimize losses resulting from exchange rate fluctuations, while customers are assured that transportation costs remain within a predictable range.

CBM (Cubic Meter)

CBM is a unit of volume that represents the space of a cube measuring 1 meter x 1 meter x 1 meter. This unit is primarily used in the logistics and transportation sectors to measure the volume of cargo, playing a crucial role in calculating transportation costs in international trade. CBM is an essential indicator for assessing cargo capacity and space efficiency in maritime, air, and land transportation. This measurement enables carriers to optimize logistics planning and accurately estimate transportation costs for customers.

CBR (Critical Bunker Recovery)

CBR refers to the additional charge imposed by maritime carriers due to sharp increases in fuel prices or instability in fuel supply. This surcharge is established by airlines and shipping companies to compensate for fluctuations in fuel costs, becoming effective when fuel prices exceed a certain level. The critical bunker recovery charge helps manage the economic risks that may arise in logistics and transportation contracts, contributing to the maintenance of stable transportation services. This allows carriers to minimize losses resulting from rising fuel costs while ensuring that customers can utilize cargo transportation services at predictable costs.

CCF (Collect Charge Fee)

CCF refers to an additional charge typically imposed by freight forwarders in air transportation when the freight for incoming cargo is to be paid on delivery. This fee, ranging from 2% to 5%, is applied to manage payment transfers or currency risks associated with the originating country. It acts as a form of currency conversion fee and includes the costs that the importer must pay to receive the cargo.

CCF (Container Cleaning Fee)

CCF refers to the charges incurred when cleaning a container is required before or after loading, depending on the nature of the cargo. This fee is applicable when the interior of the container needs to be kept clean, particularly in situations where specific types of cargo require special storage or transportation. The container cleaning fee arises when the carrier provides cleaning services or hires an external company to clean the container, ensuring that the customer receives their cargo in a clean container. Related terminology includes CCC (Container Cleaning Charge), which plays a crucial role in maintaining the quality of goods in international trade.

CFR (Cost and Freight)

CFR refers to the shipping term under which the seller is responsible for the cost of the goods and the freight to transport the goods to the destination port. Under this condition, the seller bears not only the price of the goods but also the shipping costs, while the risk transfers to the buyer once the goods are loaded onto the vessel. This arrangement helps exporters manage costs incurred during transportation and allows buyers to predict the total costs, including shipping, in advance. CFR is one of the commonly used trade terms in international trade, playing a crucial role in ensuring the safe delivery of goods and the smooth progression of transactions.

CFS (Container Freight Station)

CFS refers to a facility that consolidates and handles containerized cargo, primarily focusing on the unloading, storage, and sorting of import and export shipments. At this location, containers are discharged from vessels, cargo is classified and relocated to appropriate transportation means, and customs clearance procedures are carried out as necessary. CFS plays a crucial role in enhancing the efficiency of logistics management and ensuring the safe movement of cargo. It acts as a link between exporters and importers, facilitating smooth cargo flow and contributing to cost reductions.

CGT (Compensated Gross Tonnage)

CGT refers to a measurement used in the shipbuilding industry, introduced in 1967 to provide a more accurate evaluation of ships as the types and designs became more complex. Unlike the traditional Gross Tonnage (GT), CGT incorporates factors such as processing hours, equipment capabilities, and ship prices that GT cannot adequately represent. CGT is calculated using a relative index, known as the CGT coefficient, based on a baseline of 15,000 DWT (10,000 GT) general cargo ships, where the construction workload (processing hours) required per GT is set at 1.0. The CGT coefficient is established for each type and design of ship, and the CGT is obtained by multiplying this coefficient with the ship's GT.

CI (Commercial Invoice)

CI refers to a document that records the details of a transaction related to the sale of goods, specifying the terms between the seller and the buyer. This document includes information such as the type, quantity, and price of the goods, payment terms, and shipping method, playing an essential role in international trade. The commercial invoice is a crucial document required for customs clearance and international transportation, which the importer must submit to clear the goods through customs. It serves as proof of the transaction, allowing the buyer to confirm the amount to be paid, while the seller uses it for financial management.

CIF (Cost Insurance and Freight)

CIF refers to a condition in which the seller is responsible for the cost, freight, and insurance of the goods being transported to the destination port. Under this condition, the seller bears the transportation and insurance costs in addition to the price of the goods, while the risk transfers to the buyer once the goods are shipped. The CIF condition provides additional security for the buyer, as the seller insures the goods against loss or damage, allowing the buyer to anticipate the total costs in advance.

CLC (Confirmed Letter of Credit)

CLC refers to a type of letter of credit where a third bank provides additional assurance of payment after the exporter accepts the letter of credit issued by the importer. In this case, the third bank guarantees payment to the exporter alongside the importer's bank, enhancing the security for the exporter. Confirmed letters of credit are crucial in international trade for increasing transaction reliability and reducing the exporter's risk. They are especially useful when the creditworthiness of the trading partner is low or uncertain, allowing the exporter to have confidence that the transaction will proceed smoothly.

CO (Certificate of Origin)

CO is a document that certifies the country or region in which a specific product was produced. This certificate is issued by the exporter and is required by the customs authorities of the importing country to verify the origin of the goods. The certificate of origin plays a crucial role in determining taxes, customs duties, trade regulations, and in applying differentiated benefits based on the origin. It enhances transparency in international trade and ensures that the product complies with the regulations and agreements of the respective country.

COD (Cash on Delivery)

COD is a payment method where the buyer pays for the goods in cash upon receipt. This method is widely used in online shopping and freight transportation, allowing the buyer to pay only after the product arrives. Cash on delivery enhances transaction security since the buyer can verify the product before making the payment. This approach is especially useful in dealings with unreliable counterparts, as it allows consumers to avoid prepayment, positively influencing their purchasing decisions.

CONSOL (Consolidation)

CONSOL refers to the process of combining multiple small shipments into a single large shipment for transportation. This process is primarily used in maritime and air transport, where cargo collected from various shippers is loaded together to enhance transportation efficiency. Consolidation helps reduce logistics costs and increase the frequency of transportation, making it a more economical option for shipping small quantities of cargo.

CP (Charter Party)

CP is a legal document that outlines the terms of a vessel's charter, defining the agreement between the ship owner and the charterer. This contract includes detailed information about the duration of the vessel's operation, freight rates, types of cargo, responsibilities, and obligations, and is primarily used in maritime transportation. The charter party serves to clarify all conditions of the vessel's rental, thereby preventing disputes between the parties and enhancing the safety of the transaction.

CPFR (Collaborative Planning Forecasting Replenishment)

CPFR refers to the process of collaboratively planning demand forecasting and inventory replenishment among multiple companies. This approach emphasizes sharing information among supply chain participants and jointly developing plans to enhance efficiency and minimize inventory costs. Collaborative demand forecasting utilizes real-time data and market insights to respond promptly to demand fluctuations, thereby enabling companies to meet customer needs more accurately.

CPT (Carriage Paid To)

CPT refers to the condition where the seller bears the transportation costs and delivers the goods to a specified destination. Under this condition, the seller pays for the shipping costs, while the risk transfers to the buyer when the goods are handed over to the carrier. The CPT condition offers advantages such as ensuring safe transportation of the goods by the seller and allowing the buyer to predict the total costs in advance. In contrast, CIF (Cost, Insurance, and Freight) entails the seller covering the costs of the goods, freight, and insurance to the destination, with the risk transferring to the buyer upon shipment. While CPT involves the seller covering only transportation costs to the specified destination, the risk is transferred to the buyer once the goods are handed over to the carrier. Insurance is not included in CPT, meaning the seller only bears the transportation costs, and the buyer must arrange for insurance separately if needed.

CT (Container Terminal)

CT refers to a facility designed for the unloading, storage, and distribution of containerized cargo, primarily located at ports. This terminal is equipped with the necessary equipment and infrastructure to efficiently handle large volumes of containers swiftly. It serves as a temporary storage location for cargo after it is unloaded from vessels and before it is transported inland by trucks or trains.

CW (Chargeable Weight)

CW refers to the weight used by carriers to calculate freight charges, based on the greater value between the actual weight and the volume weight of the cargo. In cases where the actual weight is less than the volume weight, the volume weight is applied, ensuring a fairer calculation of transportation costs. Chargeable weight is primarily utilized in air and sea transport, reflecting how the size and shape of the cargo can affect shipping costs.

CY (Container Yard)

CY refers to a designated outdoor area for storing and handling containerized cargo, typically located at ports or logistics centers. This facility plays a crucial role in managing the arrival and departure of cargo, as it is where containers are unloaded, loaded, and stored. The container yard serves as a storage area for containers before they are shipped by carriers and prepares them for transportation to inland destinations via trucks or trains.

DC (Demurrage Charge)

DC refers to the fees incurred when cargo is not unloaded within the specified timeframe, causing containers or vessels to remain at the port for an extended period. This charge is typically billed by the ship owner or freight carrier, and it must be paid by the cargo receiver to compensate for the losses resulting from the unloading delay.

DC (Detention Charge)

DC refers to the additional fees incurred when cargo is not unloaded from the transport vehicle within the specified timeframe and is stored for an extended period. This charge is primarily paid by the user of the truck, vessel, or container to compensate for the losses resulting from the unloading delay.

DC (Drayage Charge)

DC refers to the costs incurred when a container is transported from the port to its final destination inland. This fee is typically charged when a container is moved from the port to nearby warehouses, logistics centers, or other modes of transportation using trucks or trains.

DD (Demand Draft)

DD refers to a type of check issued by a bank that allows the payee to receive a specified amount immediately. Typically, the demand draft is issued after the payer has deposited the amount in advance, enabling the payee to exchange it for cash directly at the bank.

DDC (Destination Delivery Charge)

DDC refers to the cost incurred for delivering cargo to the recipient after it arrives at its final destination. This fee is primarily associated with the unloading, storage, and final transportation of the cargo, and it is charged by the carrier to the recipient.

DDP (Delivered Duty Paid)

DDP refers to the condition where the seller is responsible for transporting the cargo to the destination, covering all transportation costs as well as any taxes and customs duties applicable in the importing country. Under this condition, the seller bears all expenses and assumes all risks and responsibilities until the cargo reaches the buyer. The DDP terms ensure that the buyer does not incur any additional costs or liabilities upon receipt of the cargo, and the seller must pay all taxes and duties in advance.

DDU (Delivered Duty Unpaid)

DDU refers to the condition where the seller is responsible for transporting the cargo to the destination but does not pay the import duties and taxes applicable in the importing country. In this case, the seller covers all transportation costs until the cargo arrives at the destination, while the buyer is responsible for any taxes and customs duties incurred in the importing country. The DDU terms require the buyer to handle the taxes and duties directly, serving as a method of sharing risks and costs in international transactions. DDU facilitates smoother logistics by clearly delineating responsibilities between sellers and buyers regarding transportation and customs obligations.

DEQ (Delivered Ex Quay)

DEQ refers to the condition where the seller delivers the goods at the quay (wharf) of the destination. Under this condition, the seller is responsible for all transportation costs until the goods arrive at the quay, and the risk is also borne by the seller. However, once the goods reach the quay, the buyer is responsible for customs clearance and any associated costs. The DEQ terms enhance the reliability of the transaction by ensuring the safe transportation of goods by the seller, while allowing the buyer to directly receive the items.

DES (Delivered Ex Ship)

DES refers to the condition where the seller delivers the goods to the buyer directly from the ship. Under this condition, the seller bears all transportation costs and risks until the goods arrive at the destination port. The buyer assumes responsibility once the goods are unloaded from the ship.

DGR (Dangerous Goods Regulations)

DGR refers to a document that defines the regulations and guidelines for the safe transportation of hazardous materials or goods. Established by the International Air Transport Association (IATA) and other relevant agencies, these regulations include procedures and requirements for the safe handling, storage, and transportation of such cargo. The DGR details the classification, packaging, labeling, and documentation requirements for hazardous materials, contributing to the prevention of accidents and minimizing risks to people and property.

DLC (Documentary Letter of Credit)

DLC refers to a type of letter of credit issued by a bank on behalf of the importer to guarantee payment to the exporter upon the submission of specified documents. This credit mechanism enhances the safety of transactions, allowing exporters to secure payment by presenting required documents (e.g., invoices, shipping documents, insurance certificates). The structure of a DLC ensures that payment is made only if the submitted documents meet the specified requirements, thereby providing transaction security. Since payment is contingent upon the legitimacy of the documents, the buyer can verify that the products have been properly shipped and insured before making payment. Moreover, because the bank guarantees payment, exporters can receive their funds securely regardless of the creditworthiness of the trading partner. This is especially useful in dealings with partners where trust may be lacking. Additionally, DLC serves as an important tool for managing various risks that can arise in international trade, being adaptable to the laws and practices of different countries. Through these characteristics, DLC plays a crucial role in enhancing the reliability of transactions and supporting smooth cash flow in global commerce.

DO (Delivery Order)
DO refers to a document submitted by the consignee to the carrier or warehouse to receive cargo. This document is used to assert the consignee's ownership of the cargo and streamline the process of receiving it. The delivery order includes details such as the type and quantity of the cargo, the method of transportation, and the consignee's information. By presenting this document, the consignee can safely take possession of the cargo.

DP (Document against Payment)
DP refers to a payment method in which the collecting bank and the importer exchange a bill of exchange and shipping documents for cash.

In this method, a sight draft is issued, and the buyer receives the shipping documents upon payment. The document against payment allows the exporter to retain the shipping documents until the buyer pays, providing a crucial financial tool for safely conducting the transaction.

DS (Docking Survey)
DS refers to an inspection conducted before a vessel enters a dock for maintenance or repairs. This survey evaluates the structural integrity and mechanical condition of the ship to identify areas that require repair and to ensure that the vessel can operate safely. The docking survey is typically a crucial stage in the vessel's maintenance cycle, securing the safety of the ship and helping to reduce long-term operational costs. Additionally, these inspections are essential for meeting the requirements of insurers and regulatory bodies.

DWT (Dead Weight Tonnage)
DWT refers to the maximum weight a vessel can safely carry, representing the total weight of cargo, fuel, crew, and other equipment. This value is a crucial factor in assessing the vessel's loading capacity and is used to measure the efficiency of maritime transport. It impacts the design and operational performance of the ship and contributes to ensuring safety and cost-effectiveness in maritime logistics.

EBS (Emergency Bunker Surcharge)
EBS is an additional cost imposed by shipping companies due to sudden fluctuations in fuel prices or supply shortages. This surcharge is implemented to compensate for losses incurred from rising fuel costs and typically comes into effect when fuel prices exceed a certain level.

ECA (Export Credit Agency)

ECA is a government-supported institution that provides financial assistance and guarantees to exporters, helping them facilitate transactions in overseas markets and minimize risks. These agencies primarily offer export credits to help exporters reduce foreign exchange risk and enhance competitiveness. Export credit agencies lend funds or provide guarantees to exporters and also offer insurance for overseas investments, supporting exporters in achieving stable international expansion.

EL (Export License)

EL is a permit issued by government authorities that allows specific goods or technologies to be exported overseas. This license ensures that exports comply with national laws and regulations, aiming to protect national security, foreign policy, and economic interests. Export licenses may be required based on specific items, exporting countries, and trading partners, enabling the government to manage the safety of exports and regulatory compliance.

EOC (Error and Omission Clause)

EOC refers to professional liability insurance that provides coverage for errors or omissions that may occur in the services rendered by professionals. This insurance protects professionals such as lawyers, accountants, and engineers from legal liabilities they may face. It pays out compensation for damages that arise during the provision of services, enabling professionals to manage uncertain legal risks and offer more reliable services to their clients.

ETA (Estimated Time of Arrival)

ETA refers to the expected time at which cargo or passengers are anticipated to arrive at their destination. This information is crucial in logistics management as well as air and sea transportation, and it is used for planning transportation and providing customers with accurate arrival times.

ETD (Estimated Time of Departure)

ETD refers to the expected time at which cargo or passengers are anticipated to depart. This information is essential in logistics management as well as air and sea transportation, playing a crucial role in transportation planning and scheduling.

EXW (Ex-Work)

EXW refers to a transaction condition where the seller delivers the goods at their premises (factory, warehouse, etc.), and all subsequent costs and risks are borne by the buyer. Under this condition, the seller is only obligated to prepare the product for pickup, without any further responsibilities, while the buyer is responsible for receiving the goods and handling all aspects of transportation. This condition can increase the complexity of the transaction as the buyer must undertake all necessary procedures to receive the goods. Therefore, the seller's responsibility is limited to delivering the product at their location, with the buyer assuming all subsequent costs (such as transportation, insurance, customs fees, etc.).

FAF (Fuel Adjustment Factor)

FAF refers to an additional charge imposed by carriers to reflect fluctuations in fuel costs. This surcharge is commonly used in maritime, air, and land transportation, and it is passed on to customers when fuel prices rise. The fuel adjustment factor helps carriers minimize losses due to increased fuel expenses and provides customers with predictable transportation costs.

FAS (Free Alongside Ship)

FAS refers to a shipping term where the seller is responsible for delivering the goods next to the vessel at a designated port. Under this condition, the seller places the cargo alongside the ship, after which all costs and risks are transferred to the buyer. The FAS condition increases the complexity of the transaction, as the buyer must handle all procedures necessary to load the goods onto the ship.

FC (Forwarding Company)

FC refers to a business that provides international logistics and transportation services, managing all processes related to the export and import of goods as well as domestic transport. This company plans optimal transportation routes according to customer needs, handles necessary paperwork, and facilitates smooth logistics operations. Forwarding companies offer services such as transportation, warehousing, customs clearance, insurance, and cargo tracking, helping customers manage complex logistics processes more easily.

FCA (Free Carrier)

FCA refers to a condition where the seller delivers the goods to the carrier at a specified location. Under this condition, the seller is responsible for handing over the goods to the carrier, and all subsequent costs and risks are borne by the buyer. The FCA condition ensures that the seller safely delivers the goods, while the buyer must manage any risks that may arise during the transportation process.

FCL (Full Container Load)

FCL refers to a condition where a single container is filled entirely with the cargo of one customer. This method is primarily used for transporting bulk cargo, allowing the customer to exclusively use the entire container, which helps manage transportation costs more efficiently. FCL maximizes the container's loading capacity, offering advantages such as reduced logistics costs and ensuring safe transportation.

FEU (Forty-foot Equivalent Units)

FEU refers to a cargo capacity unit based on a 40-foot container. This unit is used in maritime transportation to measure the capacity of containers and is widely utilized in logistics and international trade alongside the 20-foot container unit (TEU).

FIATA (International Federation of Freight Forwarders Associations)

FIATA is an international organization representing freight forwarders and logistics-related companies worldwide. The association promotes the development of the freight transportation industry and cooperation among member countries while working to standardize global logistics and supply chain management. FIATA helps address issues faced by freight forwarders and logistics companies and contributes to enhancing the professionalism of the industry by providing education and training programs.

FIFO (First In First Out)

FIFO is a method used in inventory management and accounting, which means that the goods that are received first are the ones that are dispatched first. This method is particularly effective for managing inventory of perishable items, such as food and pharmaceuticals, where freshness is crucial. FIFO helps maintain the freshness of stock and prevents older inventory from being distributed. Additionally, it is utilized in accounting to provide a more accurate reflection of costs associated with inventory valuation.

FL (Freight List)

FL is a document that lists information related to the rates for services provided by carriers. This list includes freight rates for various types of cargo, loading conditions, transport routes, and other associated costs, serving as a useful reference for customers when selecting transportation services. The FL helps customers compare different shipping options and plan their budgets, contributing to transparent pricing and building trust between customers and carriers.

FO (Firm Offer)

FO refers to a proposal made by a seller to provide goods or services at a specified price and under certain conditions. If the recipient accepts, the offer remains unchanged for a specified period, during which the seller is obligated to uphold the stated conditions.

FOB (Free On Board)

FOB refers to a transaction condition where the seller assumes all costs and risks until the goods are loaded onto the ship at the port of shipment. Under this condition, the seller is responsible for everything until the goods are placed on board, at which point the risk transfers to the buyer. The FOB condition ensures that the seller guarantees the safe transportation of the goods, while the buyer is responsible for all costs and risks after loading.

FSC (Fuel Surcharge)

FSC refers to an additional fee charged by carriers to customers based on fluctuations in fuel costs. This surcharge is primarily applied in maritime, air, and ground transportation, and it accounts for the increased costs that carriers incur when fuel prices rise.

FT (Free Time)

FT refers to the period during which cargo can be stored at a carrier or warehouse without incurring additional charges after its arrival. This timeframe allows customers to hold their goods without extra costs, and it is typically set based on the time required for unloading and preparing the cargo for transport. Free time helps ensure that customers have sufficient time to receive their goods while also aiding carriers in managing logistics efficiently.

FTA (Free Trade Agreement)

FTA refers to an agreement between two or more countries aimed at reducing or eliminating tariffs and trade barriers on each other's goods and services. These agreements are designed to promote trade and enhance economic cooperation, increasing market access for the participating countries. Free trade agreements contribute to lowering import and export costs, improving competitiveness, and fostering economic growth.

GA (General Average)

GA refers to the principle of equitably sharing losses that occur during maritime transport among all parties involved. According to this principle, if specific cargo is deliberately damaged or lost to ensure the safety of the vessel, all cargo owners must share that loss. General average clarifies the responsibilities between ship owners and cargo owners, helping to distribute financial burdens fairly in unexpected accidents or crisis situations. Ultimately, this principle promotes cooperation and mutual support among stakeholders in maritime operations, ensuring a fair approach to risk management.

GATT (General Agreement on Tariffs and Trade)

GATT is an international agreement established in 1947 to promote global trade and reduce trade barriers among countries. This agreement regulates taxes and tariffs applicable to the export and import of goods, aiming to ensure fairness in trade and enhance economic cooperation. GATT has served as a crucial foundation for facilitating freer and fairer trade among member countries and evolved into the WTO (World Trade Organization) in 1995.

GCA (Ground Controlled Approach)

GCA refers to a navigation support system provided from the ground before an aircraft lands. This system assists the aircraft's approach through radar and voice instructions from the airport control tower, enabling safe landings even in adverse weather conditions or poor visibility. Ground Controlled Approach enhances the safety of the landing process by continuously monitoring the aircraft's position and altitude, providing pilots with the necessary information.

GL (Germanischer Lloyd)

GL is an organization that provides quality assurance and certification for the design, construction, and maintenance of ships. Established in Germany in 1867, this institution plays a crucial role in enhancing the safety of the maritime industry by establishing regulations for ships and offshore structures and inspecting compliance with these standards.

GPI (Ground Position Indicator)

GPI is a device that displays the ground position of an aircraft, primarily used in airport and flight operations management systems. This equipment helps to identify the real-time location of the aircraft on runways and taxiways, playing a crucial role in allowing pilots and air traffic controllers to confirm the aircraft's exact position.

GPWS (Ground Proximity Warning System)

GPWS is a safety system that warns pilots when an aircraft is in danger of approaching the ground or obstacles too closely. This system monitors real-time data on the aircraft's altitude, speed, and descent rate, and immediately sends warning signals when dangerous proximity to the ground is detected. The ground proximity warning system is particularly crucial in ensuring safe aircraft operations during adverse weather or low visibility conditions, providing pilots with vital information to avoid the risk of ground collision.

GRI (General Rate Increase)

GRI refers to the action taken by shipping companies to increase overall freight rates in response to rising transportation costs. This increase is typically applied uniformly to all routes or specific routes at a set point in time, influenced by factors such as fuel costs, operating expenses, and increased demand. GRI is utilized as a measure for shipping companies to maintain profitability and ensure the continued quality of their services.

GT (Gross Tonnage)

GT is a unit used to measure the total volume of a ship, serving as an indicator of its size and capacity. It includes all internal spaces of the vessel, calculated based on the hull's volume, and accounts for areas for cargo, passengers, engine rooms, and crew accommodations. GT is a crucial basis for determining shipping rates, port fees, and taxes, and it is utilized in the maritime industry to compare and evaluate the sizes of vessels.

H&M (Hull & Machinery Insurance)

H&M is an insurance policy that compensates for damages or losses to a ship's hull and machinery. This insurance is primarily taken out to protect vessels from risks such as collisions, fires, and natural disasters that may occur during maritime transport. Hull insurance plays a crucial role in reducing the financial burden on ship owners and helps prepare for unexpected losses.

HC (Handling Charge)

HC refers to the service fees incurred during the transportation, unloading, and storage of cargo. This charge includes costs associated with the movement and management of goods, such as personnel, equipment usage, and administrative processing, making it an essential expense in the logistics process.

IACS (International Association of Classification Societies)

IACS is an international organization where major classification societies worldwide collaborate to establish standards and regulations for maritime safety and environmental protection. It sets criteria for ship design, construction, and operation, ensuring member compliance to enhance safety within the maritime industry.

IC (Inspection Certificate)

IC is a document certifying that a product meets specified quality and standards, widely used in international trade to ensure trust. Issued by certified inspection bodies, it confirms the product's condition, specifications, and quality, giving both buyer and seller confidence in transaction quality. The inspection certificate serves as a vital tool in facilitating smooth trade relationships and ensuring compliance with international regulations.

ICD (Inland Container Depot)

ICD is an inland facility for container storage and handling, where various logistics operations are carried out before maritime cargo moves inland. By processing storage, customs clearance, unloading, and quarantine away from congested ports, ICDs improve efficiency, allowing import/export procedures to be managed without port visits, saving logistics costs and time.

ID (Import Declaration)

ID is the procedure of declaring imported goods to customs, detailing the type, quantity, and value of the items. This document allows customs to assess duties and ensure regulatory compliance, serving as a mandatory submission for all imports to secure lawful distribution and accurate tax and duty payments.

IL (Import License)

IL is an authorization granted by a government or relevant authority to import specific goods from abroad. Required for regulating and controlling the import of certain items, it aims to protect national security and the economy. IL is crucial for importing sensitive or security-related products, helping importers avoid legal issues and ensuring safe transactions by allowing the government to control import volumes and protect domestic industries.

ILC (Irrevocable Letter of Credit)

ILC is a credit instrument that cannot be altered or canceled without the issuing bank's consent once issued. It guarantees payment to the exporter under the agreed terms, ensuring stable receipt of funds. Widely used in international trade, this letter of credit enhances trust and transaction stability, providing legal security and protection for both exporters and importers by assuring reliable payment.

ILS (Instrument Landing System)

ILS is a navigation system that aids aircraft in precise runway approaches, providing pilots with location and angle data via groundtransmitted radio signals. Essential for safe landings in low visibility or adverse weather, ILS guides both horizontal and vertical approaches, significantly enhancing landing safety.

IMDG (International Maritime Dangerous Goods)

IMDG Code is a regulatory framework by the International Maritime Organization (IMO) for the safe handling, packaging, labeling, and transportation of hazardous materials by sea. It classifies various dangerous goods, such as explosives, toxic, and corrosive substances, ensuring safety in maritime transport by preventing accidents and enabling consistent oversight and management of hazardous cargo.

IMO (International Maritime Organization)

IMO is a United Nations agency established to enhance global maritime safety, security, and environmental protection. It sets international standards and regulations for maritime safety, pollution prevention, and port security, providing member nations with conventions and guidelines to reduce maritime accidents, prevent pollution, and improve transport efficiency and safety globally.

INCOTERMS (International Rules for the Interpretation of Trade Terms)

INCOTERMS are guidelines by the International Chamber of Commerce (ICC) that clarify the responsibilities, costs, and risks between sellers and buyers in international trade. Defining terms like EXW (Ex Works), FOB (Free on Board), and CIF (Cost, Insurance, and

Freight), INCOTERMS standardize obligations across transactions, reducing confusion and legal disputes globally. Used worldwide, these terms enable sellers and buyers to divide costs and responsibilities transparently in contract agreements and are periodically updated by the ICC to reflect evolving trade practices.

IP (Insurance Policy)

IP is an official document detailing the terms of an insurance contract between the policyholder and the insurer. It specifies coverage scope, compensation conditions, insured items, and premium payment terms, serving as the basis for claims in case of an insured event. This document clarifies the protection available to the policyholder, providing legal validity and financial security against unexpected incidents or losses while setting clear terms for the insurer's obligations.

IPI (Interior Point Intermodal)

IPI is a multimodal transport method where cargo is moved from ports to inland destinations using rail or truck following sea transit. This service combines various transport modes to efficiently deliver goods from port to final inland locations, optimizing transit time and reducing costs. In the U.S., cargo arriving at ports like Los Angeles or Long Beach from Asia is transported by rail or truck to cities such as Chicago, Dallas, or Atlanta, benefiting from a streamlined approach that reduces logistics expenses and transit durations.

IS (Intermediate Survey)

IS is an inspection conducted within a specified period before a ship's periodic survey to verify its safety and seaworthiness. This survey assesses the condition of key structures, machinery, and safety equipment, ensuring compliance with regulations and confirming the vessel's ongoing suitability for operations. It preemptively identifies potential issues and enables maintenance as needed, enhancing the ship's safety standards.

KIFFA (Korea International Freight Forwarders Association)

KIFFA represents Korean freight forwarding and logistics companies, supporting the advancement of international freight transport and logistics industries. The association promotes collaboration among members, offering training, research, and policy support to enhance industry standardization and competitiveness. KIFFA aims to boost Korea's logistics sector's global competitiveness, advocates for trade-promoting policies, and assists members in delivering safe and efficient logistics services.

LC (Letter of Credit)

LC is a financial instrument issued by a bank at the importer's request to guarantee payment to the exporter. It ensures that the bank will pay the exporter on behalf of the importer upon fulfillment of the transaction terms, enhancing payment reliability in international trade. By securing payment upon submission of shipment documents, an LC reduces risk for both trading parties, ensuring safe transactions. LC facilitates smoother international trade operations by providing assurance to exporters and enabling importers to manage their cash flow effectively.

LCL (Less than Container Load)

LCL refers to a shipping method where multiple shippers consolidate small shipments into a single container. This allows shared container use, reducing costs for international transport by distributing expenses among multiple shippers. Common among small importers and exporters, LCL enables cost savings and efficient logistics, as each shipper pays only for their cargo's portion of the container.

LG (Letter of Guarantee)

LG is a document issued by an importer to receive goods before the Bill of Lading (BL) arrives. This guarantee allows the importer to claim the goods without the BL, with the issuing bank assuring the exporter against potential losses. The LG minimizes logistics delays by enabling prompt cargo collection when the BL is not yet available.

LI (Letter of Indemnity)

LI is a document that guarantees compensation by the carrier or related parties to the consignee for damaged or lost goods during transit. It holds the carrier accountable for cargo condition or losses, fostering trust between the carrier and consignee. LI helps minimize disputes over cargo damage, ensuring smooth transaction flow.

LTA (Long Term Agreement)

LTA is a contract between a shipper and carrier to transport cargo consistently over a set period. This agreement enables stable service by pre-determining transport costs, service terms, and volume, fostering long-term cooperation. LTAs are commonly used by large shippers or companies requiring regular logistics, ensuring cost savings and reliable transport schedules.

MBL (Master Bill of Landing)

MBL is an official document issued by the shipping carrier detailing the cargo's transport route, origin, destination, and cargo information. It serves as a legal basis, holding the carrier accountable for receiving and transporting the cargo, essential for managing the logistics flow. Typically issued per a contract with a freight forwarder or direct exporter/importer, the MBL grants the final consignee the authority to claim the cargo.

MCI (Marine Cargo Insurance)

MCI is coverage that compensates for losses or damage to cargo during sea transport. It protects the shipper by covering financial losses from various risks (natural disasters, accidents, theft), reducing transport risks and enhancing stability in international trade by safeguarding against unforeseen incidents.

MF (Manifest)

MF is an official document listing all cargo on a ship or aircraft, detailing cargo specifics such as type, quantity, and destination. It assists customs and port authorities in efficiently processing transport and clearance, facilitating cargo management and tracking, and enhancing transparency and efficiency in international trade.

MFCS (Manifest Consolidation System)

MFCS is a system that consolidates multiple individual manifests into a single, unified manifest. This integration streamlines the review and customs clearance processes for customs and port authorities by combining cargo information from various shippers and carriers, enhancing efficiency in cargo handling and oversight.

MLB (Mini Land Bridge)

MLB is an intermodal transport method where cargo from Asia arrives at a U.S. West Coast port and then crosses the North American continent by rail or truck to an East Coast port. From there, it continues by sea to its final destination, such as Europe, offering an efficient route that combines land and sea transport across North

America.

MLC (Master Letter of Credit)

MLC is a credit instrument issued by a bank to secure transactions between exporters and importers in global trade, often used when multiple transactions or sub-letters of credit are required. Common in high-credit trade arrangements, the MLC guarantees payments, reducing risk in international transactions and facilitating secure and stable trade, especially in complex or large-scale transactions.

MR (Mate's Receipt)

MR is a document issued by the ship's officer to confirm that cargo has been loaded onto the vessel. It serves as initial proof of loading and forms the basis for preparing the Bill of Lading (BL) after loading completion.

MT (Metric Ton)

MT is a weight unit equivalent to 1,000 kilograms (kg), commonly used in bulk cargo and international logistics. It is widely employed for measuring raw materials, agricultural products, and energy resources, recognized globally as a standardized weight unit.

MTO (Multimodal Transport Operator)

MTO is a logistics provider that manages cargo transport to its final destination through a single contract using multiple transportation modes, such as sea, air, rail, and road. MTOs streamline the logistics process in international trade by consolidating services like transport contracts, documentation, insurance, and customs, thereby reducing complexity and optimizing both transit time and costs. MTOs enhance the efficiency of supply chains, making it easier for businesses to navigate the complexities of global logistics.

MV (Mother Vessel)

MV refers to a large ship that handles major sea routes, transporting bulk cargo over long international distances. Operating primarily between hub ports, the MV transfers cargo to smaller feeder vessels for delivery to final destinations, enhancing efficiency in bulk transport and managing cargo volumes in global logistics.

NLC (Negotiation Letter of Credit)

NLC is a credit instrument allowing exporters to present shipping documents to a bank to receive early payment. Upon document submission, the bank reviews and forwards them to the importer's bank to recover the final payment, providing the exporter with quicker fund access and enhancing cash flow—a widely used tool in international trade.

NVOCC (Non Vessel Operating Common Carrier)

NVOCC is a carrier that, despite not owning vessels, contracts to transport cargo and arranges shipping services. Acting as an intermediary between shippers and vessel-owning carriers, NVOCCs secure cargo space, issue Bills of Lading, and provide efficient, flexible transport services. They are vital in supporting seamless cargo movement, especially for smaller shippers, by simplifying the complexities of international logistics.

OA (Open Account)

OA is a payment method where the importer remits payment after receiving the goods, typically after an agreed credit period. This arrangement, favorable to the importer, is commonly used in international trade with trusted partners, as it allows deferred payment while the exporter assumes the collection risk, potentially aiding in customer retention and transaction convenience.

OBL (Original Bill of Lading)

OBL is the original document proving cargo shipment, indicating ownership and granting the consignee rights to claim the cargo. It details the transport route and cargo condition, confirming secure delivery from exporter to importer, and is essential for the cargo release process in international trade, required for the importer to take possession.

ODM (Original Development/Design Manufacturing)

ODM is a production model where manufacturers design and develop products independently and produce them upon request for other brands. The manufacturer manages the entire process from development to production, while the final brand applies its label for sale. ODM benefits brands by reducing development costs and time, and it allows manufacturers to generate revenue from self-developed products. Widely used in industries like electronics and apparel, ODM is essential for product supply and brand expansion in international markets.

OEM (Original Equipment Manufacturing)

OEM is a production model where manufacturers produce goods on behalf of a brand, applying the brand's label as requested. In this model, the manufacturer handles production without involvement in design, while the final product is marketed under the brand's name. OEM allows brands to obtain products without investing in production facilities and provides manufacturers with stable revenue through mass production. Common in electronics, automotive parts, and apparel, OEM plays a key role in efficient production and distribution across industries.

OF (Ocean Freight)

OF refers to the transportation cost incurred when shipping cargo via sea, determined by factors like cargo size, weight, transport distance, and specific conditions. It is a key cost in calculating export/import expenses, often outlined in trade contracts to clarify freight cost responsibilities. Ocean freight is essential in international trade, providing an economical means for transporting bulk goods such as raw materials, machinery, and large items over long distances.

OSC (Over Storage Charge)

OSC is an additional fee applied when cargo exceeds the allotted free storage period at a port, warehouse, or container yard. This charge encourages efficient cargo movement and optimal use of storage space, prompting shippers to expedite handling and adjust transportation schedules promptly, thereby enhancing logistics efficiency.

OTC (Open Top Container)

OTC is a container with an open top, ideal for loading irregularly shaped or oversized cargo. It allows top loading and unloading using cranes or other equipment, making it suitable for transporting tall equipment, large machinery, and items that don't fit in standard containers.

PA (Particular Average)

PA refers to a loss borne solely by the owner of specific cargo damaged during sea transport, due to incidents like accidents or natural disasters. Distinct from General Average (GA), PA involves no shared cost among other stakeholders, with compensation possible depending on insurance terms, making the cargo owner solely responsible for their loss.

PCS (Port Congestion Surcharge)

PCS is an extra fee applied when port congestion causes delays in docking and cargo handling. This surcharge, passed from carriers to shippers, covers additional costs from congestion and reflects the variability in transport schedules due to delays.

PL (Packing List)

PL is a document detailing the contents, quantity, weight, and packaging of export/import cargo. It serves as a reference for verifying cargo details, aiding customs and the importer in accurately inspecting and identifying the shipment.

PSS (Peak Season Surcharge)

PSS is an additional fee imposed during peak shipping seasons when demand surges. Primarily used in maritime transport, PSS addresses vessel space scarcity and port congestion during high-demand periods like summer holidays or year-end, allowing carriers to cover increased costs and prioritize cargo placement for shippers.

RIPI (Revised Interior Point Intermodal)

RIPI is an enhanced version of the IPI service, where cargo from Asia arrives at a U.S. West Coast port and is then transported via rail and road to specific inland destinations. It also includes routes where cargo transits through the Panama Canal to U.S. East Coast and Gulf ports, followed by rail and truck transport to inland areas, optimizing delivery to diverse regions.

RORO (Roll On Roll Off Vessel)

RORO is a type of ship designed to transport vehicles like cars and trucks, allowing them to drive directly onto and off the vessel via ramps. This method eliminates the need for cranes or specialized unloading equipment, reducing loading and unloading time and enabling efficient transport.

RT (Revenue Ton)

RT is a unit used to calculate freight charges based on either the weight or volume of cargo, whichever incurs a higher rate. By selecting the charge basis between weight (tons) or volume (cubic meters), this approach ensures fair and efficient cost management for carriers and fair shipping rates for shippers.

RVP (Reid Vapor Pressure)

RVP measures the volatility of liquid fuels, particularly crude oil and petroleum products, indicating the vapor pressure generated at a specified temperature (100°F or about 37.8°C). Used to assess fuel volatility, RVP helps manage vapor pressure risks during storage and transportation.

RVR (Runway Visual Range)

RVR is the maximum distance a pilot can visually identify along the runway, primarily measured based on weather conditions. Essential for safe takeoffs and landings, RVR varies with fog, rain, or snow, providing crucial information on runway visibility to pilots and air traffic controllers, determining aircraft operations in specific weather conditions. Accurate RVR measurements are vital for ensuring aviation safety and efficiency during adverse weather conditions. understanding RVR helps enhance operational decision-making in the aviation sector, ensuring the safety of both passengers and crew.

RVV (Runway Visibility Value)

RVV measures the visual distance along the runway, indicating how far a pilot can see obstacles or markers. Calculated based on visibility at specific points and influenced by weather conditions, RVV is crucial for assessing landing and takeoff safety, providing pilots and controllers with clear runway visibility information.

SBL (Surrender Bill of Lading)

SBL allows the importer to receive cargo without the original Bill of Lading by having the exporter surrender it and process electronically. This expedites cargo release upon arrival, reducing document exchange time and enhancing import efficiency, particularly beneficial for urgent shipments, minimizing document loss risks and supporting swift cargo handling in international trade.

SBL (Switch Bill of Lading)

SBL is a document issued to replace the original Bill of Lading, commonly used in trade transactions involving intermediaries. It allows the intermediary to modify or conceal details like the origin or seller information, providing only necessary information to the final buyer. SBL helps protect sensitive data and offers flexibility in managing transactions within international trade.

SC (Service Contract)

SC is a long-term agreement between a shipper and carrier to provide transport services at fixed rates and conditions over a specified period. Common for large or regular shipments, it ensures agreed rates and services, offering stable transport costs for the shipper and consistent cargo volumes for the carrier.

SC (Shipping Company)

SC is a company providing sea transport services, responsible for transporting cargo by ship. It owns or operates various vessels and, through contracts with shippers, transports raw materials, goods, and vehicles to ports worldwide. SCs play a key role in international trade by managing routes, setting freight rates, and planning logistics to ensure smooth maritime transport, also offering tailored services to meet customer needs.

SC (Shoring Charge)

SC refers to the cost associated with securing cargo on a vessel or transport vehicle to prevent movement or damage during transit. This process involves stabilizing cargo with supports or fastenings, ensuring safe transport, and is charged for items requiring special securing, such as heavy machinery or oversized cargo, to avoid damage in transit.

SCR (Specific Commodity Rate)

SCR is a special freight rate set for specific goods, differing from general cargo rates. It applies to items requiring unique handling or significant space, such as agricultural products, chemicals, or electronics, allowing shippers and carriers to establish mutually fair costs and provide more efficient transport services tailored to the cargo's characteristics.

SD (Shipping Date)

SD is the date on which cargo departs for transport, serving as a crucial timeline in contractual agreements. It determines delivery schedules and associated costs, set according to the terms between exporter and importer.

SD (Shipping Document)
SD encompasses all necessary paperwork for cargo transport, including invoices, Bills of Lading, and packing lists. Essential for export and import processes, these documents detail cargo type, quantity, price, and transport routes, enabling customs and carriers to verify and handle the shipment accurately.

SGS (Societe Generale de Surveillance)
SGS is a global inspection, verification, testing, and certification company headquartered in Switzerland, ensuring quality and standards across various industries. It performs quality control, safety validation, and regulatory compliance checks, building trust between companies and consumers.

SO (Sipping Order)
SO is an official instruction document provided to the carrier, detailing the type, quantity, and destination of cargo for shipment. It formalizes the shipper's request, supplying the carrier with essential information for accurate cargo loading and transport.

SOC (Shipper's Own Container)
SOC refers to the use of a container owned or leased by the shipper for transporting cargo. This approach saves container rental fees from the carrier, allowing the shipper greater flexibility in managing transport schedules and locations, commonly used for specialized cargo or specific transport needs. Utilizing SOC can enhance cost efficiency and operational control in the shipping process.

SR (Shipping Request)

SR is a document submitted by the shipper to the carrier, requesting cargo shipment and detailing specifics such as cargo type, quantity, destination, and shipping schedule. Essential for ensuring timely and accurate loading, the SR enables carriers to plan and prepare transport processes, enhancing logistics efficiency and clarity among all involved parties.

SSC (Security Surcharge)

SSC is an additional fee imposed to cover security-related costs in transport, helping mitigate risks such as terrorism, theft, and smuggling. This surcharge funds enhanced security measures to ensure the safe transport of cargo.

TC (Tally Charge)

TC is an additional fee for verifying the count, weight, and condition of cargo during loading and unloading. This charge supports tallying operations to ensure the cargo's integrity and accuracy in transit, especially useful for large or mixed shipments, aiding consistency and quality management in trade.

TC (Time Charter)

TC is a contract where a ship owner leases a vessel to a charterer for a set period, with the charterer covering fuel and operating expenses during that time. The ship owner provides the crew, including the captain, while the charterer manages the vessel's schedule and cargo transport, offering flexibility for trade companies needing long-term transport solutions. Time charters allow businesses to adapt their shipping needs without the long-term commitment of purchasing a vessel.

TC (Trucking Charge)

TC refers to the cost of transporting cargo by truck to its final destination, such as a port, warehouse, or factory. This charge varies based on cargo size, weight, distance, and truck type, covering the essential last leg of delivery in international logistics.

TEU (Twenty Foot Equivalent Unit)

TEU is a cargo transport unit based on a standard 20-foot (6.1-meter) container. Used by ships, ports, and cargo terminals, it serves as a standard metric for assessing container cargo capacity in international logistics, aiding efficient capacity management and planning in maritime transport by facilitating easy comparison and calculation of a vessel's load.

THC (Terminal Handling Charge)

THC is a fee for loading, unloading, moving, and storing cargo at a port or terminal. It covers the use of equipment like forklifts and cranes during cargo handling processes and is charged by port or terminal operators as part of entry and exit procedures.

TL (Total Loss)

TL refers to the complete destruction or irreparable damage of cargo, rendering it a total loss. Common in insurance, it establishes a basis for claiming full compensation, as the cargo or vessel's value is entirely lost, reducing the financial risk for shippers in trade transactions by ensuring comprehensive coverage for such losses.

TR (Trust Receipt)

TR is a document allowing an importer to receive and sell imported goods held as collateral by the bank, which temporarily retains ownership until repayment. It enables the importer to utilize the goods before full payment, supporting cash flow in international trade, especially beneficial for quick inventory turnover, and aids importers in managing operational funds effectively.

TS (Trans-shipment)

TS is the process of transferring cargo from one mode of transport to another, typically at an intermediate port, to reach its final destination. Common in international logistics, trans-shipment is essential for moving goods across multiple countries or continents.

TSCS (Trans-Siberian Container Service)

TSCS is a transport service that swiftly and efficiently moves cargo from Asia to Europe via the Trans-Siberian Railway. Combining sea and land transport, it enables cargo from Far East Asian ports to reach major European cities quickly by traversing Siberia.

TSR (Trans-Siberian Railway)

TSR is the world's longest railway, spanning approximately 9,289 kilometers across Russia from Moscow to Vladivostok. It connects Asia and Europe, serving as a vital transport route for various cargo and passengers.

TT (Telegraphic Transfer)

TT is a method of remittance through banks or financial institutions, enabling immediate fund transfers via electronic communication. Widely used in international transactions, TT requires only the payment amount and recipient details, providing a fast and secure way to transfer funds, especially beneficial for quick overseas payments.

TT (Transit Time)

TT refers to the duration taken for cargo to travel from origin to destination. A critical factor in logistics, it directly impacts transport scheduling and planning, essential for evaluating operational efficiency and providing customers with accurate delivery timelines.

TTC (Through Transport Club)

TTC is an insurance association established to cover liability for cargo loss or damage in international transport. It shares risk between carriers and shippers, offering protection against incidents that may occur during the transport process.

TVP (True Vapor Pressure)

TVP is the pressure exerted by a liquid's vapor at a given temperature, indicating how readily the liquid vaporizes. Essential in the petroleum and chemical industries, it assesses safety in storage and transport, especially for volatile chemicals or crude oil, varying with substance characteristics and environmental conditions.

TWRA (Transpacific Westbound Rate Agreement)

TWRA is an agreement to adjust freight rates for cargo transport between Asia and North America. It standardizes rates and service conditions between carriers and shippers, aiming for efficient logistics and stable transport services, enhancing cost predictability and maintaining market competitiveness.

UCP (Uniform Customs and Practice for Documentary Credits)

UCP is a standardized set of rules governing letter of credit transactions in international trade, enhancing clarity and trust between shippers and exporters. Established by the International

Chamber of Commerce (ICC), UCP provides consistency in letter of credit transactions worldwide by defining document requirements, payment terms, and other trade-related regulations, thereby promoting transparency, efficiency, and security in trade transactions.

ULC (Usance Letter of Credit)

ULC is a letter of credit allowing the importer to pay the exporter after a specified period following shipment. This provides the importer with time to receive and potentially sell the goods before payment, aiding cash flow and supporting trade flexibility, making it a valuable financial tool in international trade.

VOY (Voyage)

VOY refers to the sequence of a vessel's journey from its origin to destination, primarily used in maritime transport. It encompasses the full route, including departure, transit, and arrival, typically with the purpose of carrying specific cargo.

VSL (Vessel)

VSL refers to a maritime transport vehicle designed to carry cargo or passengers. Vessels come in various types and sizes, such as cargo ships, passenger ships, and container ships, each tailored for specific purposes and playing a crucial role in international logistics and commerce.

WA (With Average)

WA refers to an insurance condition that covers partial losses incurred during cargo transport, meaning the insurer compensates only when specific criteria for loss are met. Commonly used in marine insurance, this condition ensures that even if only part of the cargo is lost, compensation is provided, helping the shipper minimize losses.

WCS (Weight Surcharge)

WCS refers to an additional fee imposed when the weight of cargo exceeds specified limits. Typically applied in air and sea transport, this surcharge accounts for the extra transportation costs incurred due to the overweight cargo.

WFG (Wharfage)

WFG refers to the fees charged for cargo handling, loading, or storage at a port. This cost covers the operation and maintenance of the port and the use of cargo handling facilities, paid by shippers for services utilized at the port. The fee varies based on the type and quantity of cargo and the handling methods employed at the port.

WRS (War Risk Surcharge)

WRS is an additional fee imposed to cover risks associated with war, civil unrest, or terrorism during maritime transport. This surcharge is applied when shipping in areas with higher risks due to conflict or political instability, and it is included in both insurance premiums and transportation costs.

WT (Weight Ton)

WT is a unit of measurement for cargo weight, typically based on 1 ton (1,000 kilograms). This term is used in international logistics and transportation to assess the weight of cargo and determine freight charges.

Index

AAP (Age Additional Premium)	227
AB (Accepting Bank)	227
AB (Accommodation Bill)	25
AB (Advising Bank)	227
ABL (Asset Backed Loan)	25
ABS (Asset-Backed Securities)	25
AC (Account Current)	228
ACC (Air Cargo Consolidator)	228
ACT (Air Cargo Transportation)	229
ADR (European Agreement concerning the International Carriage of Dangerous Goods by Road)	229
ADS (Alternative Depreciation System)	26
AIV (Agreed Insurable Value)	230
ALB (America Land Bridge)	230
ALC (Acceptance Letter of Credit)	231
ALM (Asset Liability Management)	26
AMC (Asset Management Company)	177
AML (Anti-Money Laundering)	27
AMR (Agreed Minimum Rate)	231

AMS (Automatic Manifest System Charge)	231
AOG (Arrival of Goods)	232
AON (Accident of Navigation)	232
APM (Asset Performance Management)	177
AR (Acceptance Rate)	233
AR (Advance Remittance)	232
AR (Annual Report)	27
AS (Adverse Selection)	28
AS (Annual Survey)	233
ASF (Available Stable Funding)	28
ASR (Airport Surveillance Radar)	234
ASRS (Automated Storage and Retrieval System)	234
ATA (Actual Time of Arrival)	234
ATD (Actual Time of Departure)	235
ATL (Absolute Total Loss)	235
AWB (Air-way Bill)	236
B2B (Business to Business)	178
B2C (Business to Customer)	178

BA (Banker's Acceptance)	29
BA (Banker's Acceptance)	236
BAF (Bunker Adjustment Factor)	236
BC (Block Chain)	29
BCP (Business Continuity Plan)	179
BCR (Benefit Cost Ratio)	30
BD (Big Data)	179
BE (Bandwagon Effect)	30
BE (Base Effect)	30
BEP (Break Even Point)	31
BIS (Bank for International Settlements)	31
BL (Bill of Lading)	237
BM (Business Model)	180
BMC (Business Model Canvas)	180
BMS (Budgetary Management System)	31
BOD (Board of Directors)	181
BOP (Balance of Payments)	32
BPM (Business Process Management)	182

BPS (Book-value per Share)	32
BR (Bank Run)	33
BS (Balance Sheet)	33
BSC (Balanced Score Card)	182
BSI (Business Survey Index)	183
BW (Bond with Warrant)	34
CA (Correction Advice)	237
CAD (Cash against Documents)	237
CAF (Currency Adjustment Factor)	238
CAGR (Compound Annual Growth Rate)	183
CAPEX (Capital Expenditure)	34
CB (Circuit Breaker)	35
CB (Commercial Bank)	35
CB (Commercial Bill)	36
CB (Convertible Bond)	36
CB (Covered Bond)	36
CBM (Cubic Meter)	238
CBO (Collateralized Bond Obligation)	37

CBR (Critical Bunker Recovery)	238
CC (Credit Creation)	37
CC (Credit Crunch)	38
CCB (Contingent Convertible Bond)	38
CCF (Collect Charge Fee)	239
CCF (Container Cleaning Fee)	239
CCF (Credit Conversion Factor)	39
CCP (Central Counter Party)	39
CCSI (Composite Consumer Sentiment Index)	40
CD (Certificate of Deposit)	40
CD (Countervailing Duties)	40
CD (Credit Derivative)	41
CDD (Commercial Due Diligence)	184
CDO (Collateralized Debt Obligation)	41
CEA (Credit Equivalent Amount)	42
CET1 (Common Equity Tier 1)	42
CF (Crowd Funding)	43
CFC (Common Fund for Commodities)	43

CFP (Capital Facilities Plan)	184
CFR (Cost and Freight)	239
CFS (Cash Flow Statement)	44
CFS (Container Freight Station)	240
CGT (Compensated Gross Tonnage)	240
CI (Commercial Invoice)	241
CI (Composite Indexes of Business Indicators)	44
CIA (Certified Internal Auditor)	45
CIF (Cost Insurance and Freight)	241
CL (Credit Leverage)	45
CLC (Confirmed Letter of Credit)	241
CLN (Credit Linked Notes)	45
CLO (Collateralized Loan Obligation)	46
CM (Capital Market)	46
CMA (Cash Management Account)	47
CMO (Collateralized Mortgage Obligation)	47
CMS (Cash Management Service)	48
CMS (Credit Management System)	48

CO (Call Option)	49
CO (Certificate of Origin)	242
COD (Cash on Delivery)	242
COFIX (Cost of Funds Index)	49
COGS (Cost of Goods Sold)	50
CONSOL (Consolidation)	242
CP (Capital Productivity)	50
CP (Charter Party)	243
CP (Commercial Paper)	51
CP (Contractionary Policy)	51
CPA (Certified Public Accountant)	51
CPFR (Collaborative Planning Forecasting Replenishment)	243
CPI (Consumer Price Index)	52
CPI (Cost-Push Inflation)	52
CPT (Carriage Paid To)	243
CR (Capitalization Rate)	53
CRAs (Credit Ratings Agencies)	53
CRM (Customer Relationship Management)	185

CS (Credit Spread)	54
CS (Customer Satisfaction)	185
CSD (Central Securities Depository)	54
CSI (Consumer Survey Index)	55
CSI (Customer Satisfaction Index)	186
CSR (Corporate Social Responsibility)	186
CSS (Credit Scoring System)	55
CT (Container Terminal)	244
CW (Chargeable Weight)	244
CWM (Chain Weighted Method)	55
CY (Container Yard)	244
D&A (Depreciation and Amortization)	56
DC (Demurrage Charge)	245
DC (Detention Charge)	245
DC (Drayage Charge)	245
DCB (Dual Currency Bond)	56
DD (Demand Draft)	245
DDC (Destination Delivery Charge)	246

DDM (Dividend Discount Model)	57
DDP (Delivered Duty Paid)	246
DDU (Delivered Duty Unpaid)	246
DE (Demonstration Effect)	58
DEQ (Delivered Ex Quay)	247
DES (Delivered Ex Ship)	247
DF (Direct Financing)	58
DGR (Dangerous Goods Regulations)	247
DLC (Documentary Letter of Credit)	247
DLT (Distributed Ledger Technology)	59
DO (Delivery Order)	248
DP (Document against Payment)	248
DPI (Demand-Pull Inflation)	59
DPI (Disposable Personal Income)	60
DPL (Deposit Placement Line)	60
DR (Depositary Receipts)	61
DRP (Distribution Requirement Planning)	187
DS (Docking Survey)	249

DSCR (Debt Service Coverage Ratio)	61
DSR (Debt Service Ratio)	62
DTI (Debt to Income Ratio)	62
DVP (Delivery versus Payment)	63
DWT (Dead Weight Tonnage)	249
EAD (Exposure at Default)	64
EAM (Enterprise Asset Management)	187
EAMS (Enterprise Architecture Management System)	188
EB (Exchangeable Bond)	64
EBITDA (Earnings Before Interest, Tax, Depreciation, and Amortization)	65
EBS (Emergency Bunker Surcharge)	249
EC (Electronic Commerce)	188
EC (Executive Committee)	189
ECA (Export Credit Agency)	250
ECCS (Enterprise Controlling and Consolidation System)	189
ED (External Debt)	66
EDI (Electronic Data Interchange)	190
EEF (Exchange Equalization Fund)	66

EIS (Executive Information Systems)	190
EITC (Earned Income Tax Credit)	67
EL (Export License)	250
ELD (Equity Linked Deposit)	67
ELF (Equity Linked Fund)	68
ELS (Equity Linked Security)	69
EM (Electronic Money)	69
EMBI (Emerging Market Bond Index)	70
EMV (Expected Monetary Value)	71
EOC (Error and Omission Clause)	250
EOS (Economy of Scope)	71
EPS (Earnings per Share)	72
ERP (Enterprise Resource Planning)	190
ES (Exit Strategy)	191
ESG (Environment Social Governance)	191
ESI (Employee Satisfaction Index)	192
ESI (Export Similarity Index)	72
ETA (Estimated Time of Arrival)	250

ETD (Estimated Time of Departure)	251
ETF (Exchange Traded Fund)	73
EURIBOR (Euro Interbank Offered Rate)	74
EV (Enterprise Value)	193
EVA (Economic Value Added)	74
EXW (Ex-Work)	251
FAF (Fuel Adjustment Factor)	251
FAS (Free Alongside Ship)	252
FC (Factor Cost)	75
FC (Forward Contracts)	75
FC (Forwarding Company)	252
FCA (Free Carrier)	252
FCL (Full Container Load)	252
FD (Final Demand)	76
FD (Financial Derivatives)	76
FE (Fountain Effect)	77
FEU (Forty-foot Equivalent Units)	253
FHC (Financial Holdings Company)	193

Index | 293

FI (Financial Investor)	194
FIATA (International Federation of Freight Forwarders Associations)	253
FIFO (First In First Out)	253
FL (Freight List)	254
FM (Facility Management)	194
FMV (Fair Market Value)	195
FO (Firm Offer)	254
FOB (Free On Board)	254
FOP (Free of Payment)	78
FRM (Financial Risk Management)	195
FRN (Floating Rate Note)	78
FRS (Fractional Reserve System)	79
FS (Feasibility Study)	196
FSC (Fuel Surcharge)	254
FT (Free Time)	255
FT (Futures Transactions)	79
FTA (Free Trade Agreement)	255
FV (Face Value)	80

FWM (Fixed Weighted Method)	81
FX (Foreign Exchange)	81
GA (General Average)	255
GAAP (Generally Accepted Accounting Principles)	82
GATT (General Agreement on Tariffs and Trade)	256
GCA (Ground Controlled Approach)	256
GCF (Green Climate Fund)	196
GDI (Gross Domestic Investment Ratio)	82
GDP (Gross Domestic Product)	83
GDR (Global Depositary Receipts)	83
GDS (General Depreciation System)	84
GFCF (Gross Fixed Capital Formation)	84
GL (General Ledger)	85
GL (Germanischer Lloyd)	256
GL (Gross Loss)	85
GMA (Geometric Moving Average)	86
GNI (Gross National Income)	86
GP (General Provisions)	86

GP (Gross Profit)	87
GPI (Ground Position Indicator)	256
GPWS (Ground Proximity Warning System)	257
GRI (General Rate Increase)	257
GRI (Global Reporting Initiative)	197
GT (Gross Tonnage)	257
GT (Group Technology)	197
GVA (Gross Value Added)	87
GVC (Global Value Chain)	88
H&M (Hull & Machinery Insurance)	258
HC (Handling Charge)	258
HDI (Household Disposable Income)	89
HE (Hidden Economy)	89
HHI (Herfindahl-Hirschman Index)	90
HRD (Human Resources Development)	198
HSS (Hybrid Settlement System)	90
HTBC (Historical Trend Base Change)	198
IA (Information Asymmetry)	199

IACS (International Association of Classification Societies)	258
IB (Investment Bank)	91
IC (Inspection Certificate)	258
IC (Intermediate Consumption)	91
ICD (Inland Container Depot)	259
ICO (Initial Coin Offering)	91
ID (Import Declaration)	259
IF (Indirect Financing)	92
IFRS (International Financing Reporting Standards)	93
IL (Import License)	259
ILC (Irrevocable Letter of Credit)	259
ILG (Income-Led Growth)	93
ILS (Instrument Landing System)	260
IMDG (International Maritime Dangerous Goods)	260
IMO (International Maritime Organization)	260
INCOTERMS (International Rules for the Interpretation of Trade Terms)	260
IOT (Input-Output Tables)	94
IP (Insurance Policy)	261

IP (Intellectual Property)	199
IPI (Interior Point Intermodal)	261
IPO (Initial Public Offering)	200
IPR (Intellectual Property Rights)	200
IR (Investor Relations)	201
IRR (Internal Rate of Return)	94
IRS (Interest Rate Swaps)	95
IS (Intermediate Survey)	261
ISDS (Investor-State Dispute Settlement)	201
IT (Impossible Trinity, Impossible Trilemma)	96
JB (Junk Bond)	96
KIFFA (Korea International Freight Forwarders Association)	262
KIKO (Knock-In Knock-Out)	97
KMS (Knowledge Management System)	202
KPI (Key Performance Indicator)	202
KYC (Know Your Customer)	97
LBO (Leveraged Buy Out)	98
LC (Letter of Credit)	262

LCL (Less than Container Load)	262
LCR (Liquidity Coverage Ratio)	98
LDR (Law of Diminishing Returns)	99
LE (Leverage Effect)	99
LG (Letter of Guarantee)	263
LGD (Loss Given Default)	100
LI (Letter of Indemnity)	263
LT (Liquidity Trap)	101
LTA (Long Term Agreement)	263
LTV (Loan to Value Ratio)	101
M&A (Mergers & Acquisition)	202
M&O (Monopoly and Oligopoly)	203
MACRS (Modified Accelerated Cost Recovery System)	102
MBA (Master of Business Administration)	203
MBL (Master Bill of Landing)	263
MBO (Management by Objectives)	204
MBS (Mortgage Backed Securities)	102
MCI (Marine Cargo Insurance)	264

MF (Manifest)	264
MFCS (Manifest Consolidation System)	264
MLB (Mini Land Bridge)	264
MLC (Master Letter of Credit)	265
MMF (Money Market Fund)	103
MOS (Margin of Safety)	104
MPB (Monetary Policy Board)	104
MR (Mate's Receipt)	265
MS (Market Share)	204
MT (Metric Ton)	265
MTM (Mark to Market)	105
MTO (Multimodal Transport Operator)	265
MV (Mother Vessel)	266
MVA (Market Value Added)	106
NBD (New Business Development)	205
NCD (Negotiable Certificate of Deposit)	106
NDC (Net Debit Caps)	107
NDF (Non-Deliverable Forward)	107

NDI (National Disposable Income)	108
NEER (Nominal Effective Exchange Rate)	108
NGDP (Nominal Gross Domestic Product)	109
NGT (New Growth Theory)	109
NI (Net Income)	110
NI (Nominal Income)	111
NIM (Net Interest Margin)	112
NL (Net Loss)	112
NLC (Negotiation Letter of Credit)	266
NM (Natural Monopoly)	113
NNI (Net National Income)	113
NOC (No Occupancy Cost)	114
NOE (Non-Observed Economy)	115
NOI (Net Operating Income)	116
NP (Notional Principal)	117
NPV (Net Present Value)	117
NSFR (Net Stable Funding Ratio)	118
NVOCC (Non Vessel Operating Common Carrier)	266

O&M (Operation & Maintenance)	205
OA (Open Account)	266
OB (Offshore Banking)	119
OBL (Original Bill of Lading)	267
OBS (Organizational Breakdown Structure)	206
OC (Opportunity Cost)	206
OCC (Occupancy)	119
ODM (Original Development/Design Manufacturing)	267
OEM (Original Equipment Manufacturing)	267
OF (Ocean Freight)	268
OI (Operating Income)	120
OMO (Open Market Operation)	207
OPEX (Operating Expenditures)	121
OR (Operational Risk)	208
ORA (Official Reserve Assets)	122
OS (Operating Surplus)	122
OSC (Over Storage Charge)	268
OTC (Open Top Container)	268

OTC (Over-The-Counter)	123
PA (Particular Average)	268
PAC (Planning Advisory Committee)	123
PAM (Plant Asset Management)	208
PB (Protection Buyer)	124
PBR (Price on Book-value Ratio)	125
PCS (Port Congestion Surcharge)	269
PD (Probability of Default)	125
PDI (Personal Disposable Income)	126
PED (Price Elasticity of Demand)	126
PER (Price Earnings Ratio)	127
PF (Project Financing)	208
PFV (Project Financing Vehicle)	209
PG (Payment Gateway)	127
PI (Payment Instruments)	128
PI (Property Income)	128
PL (Packing List)	269
PL (Profit and Loss Statement)	129
PLG (Profit-Led Growth)	129
PM (Primary Market)	130

PO (Put Option)	130
PPI (Producer Price Index)	131
PPP (Purchasing Power Parity)	131
PR (Principal Risk)	132
PS (Protection Seller)	133
PSS (Peak Season Surcharge)	269
PT (Program Trading)	133
PTC (Propensity to Consume)	134
PV (Present Value)	134
PVP (Payment versus Payment)	135
QE (Qualitative Easing)	135
QE (Quantitative Easing)	136
R&D (Research and Development)	209
RB (Reserve Base)	136
RCA (Revealed Comparative Advantage)	137
RE (Ratchet Effect)	138
REER (Real Effective Exchange Rate)	138
REITs (Real Estate Investment Trust)	139
RI (Real Income)	139
RIPI (Revised Interior Point Intermodal)	269

RML (Reverse Mortgage Loan)	140
ROA (Return on Asset)	140
ROE (Return on Equity)	140
ROI (Return on Investment)	141
ROR (Return on Revenue)	141
RORO (Roll On Roll Off Vessel)	270
RP (Repurchase Agreements)	142
RPS (Retail Payment System)	142
RSF (Required Stable Funding)	143
RT (RegTech; Regulatory Technology)	143
RT (Revenue Ton)	270
RVP (Reid Vapor Pressure)	270
RVR (Runway Visual Range)	270
RVV (Runway Visibility Value)	271
RWA (Risk-Weighted Assets)	144
S&P (Standard & Poor)	144
SAP (System Application and Programs in Data Process)	145
SAS (Statistical Analysis System)	145
SB (Specialized Banking)	146
SB (Straight Bond)	146

SBL (Surrender Bill of Lading)	271
SBL (Switch Bill of Lading)	271
SC (Service Contract)	271
SC (Shipping Company)	272
SC (Shoring Charge)	272
SC (Sunk Cost)	147
SC (Supplementary Capital)	147
SCF (Sunk Cost Fallacy)	148
SCM (Supply Chain Management)	149
SCR (Specific Commodity Rate)	272
SD (Shipping Date)	272
SD (Shipping Document)	273
SDR (Special Drawing Rights)	149
SE (Snob Effect)	150
SEEA (System of Integrated Environmental and Economic Accounts)	150
SF (Settlement Finality)	151
SGS (Societe Generale de Surveillance)	273
SI (Social Insurance)	151
SI (Strategic Investor)	210
SIFIs (Systemically Important Financial Institutions)	152

SIO (Stock Index Options)	152
SM (Secondary Market)	153
SNA (System of National Accounts)	153
SO (Sipping Order)	273
SO (Smoothing Operation)	154
SO (Stock Option)	155
SOC (Shipper's Own Container)	273
SOHO (Small Office Home Office)	155
SOW (Share of Wallet)	210
SP (Sterilization Policy)	155
SPC (Special Purpose Company)	211
SPM (Strategic Performance Measurement)	211
SR (Shipping Request)	274
SR (Swap Rate)	156
SRI (Socially Responsible Investment)	212
SSC (Security Surcharge)	274
ST (Security Thread)	156
ST (Stress Test)	157
SU (Statistical Underground)	157
SUT (Supply and Use Tables)	158

SWIFT (Society of Worldwide Interbank Financial Telecommunication)	159
SWOT (Strengths, Weaknesses, Opportunities, Threats)	212
TB (Trading Book)	159
TC (Tally Charge)	274
TC (Time Charter)	274
TC (Trucking Charge)	275
TCO (Total Cost of Ownership)	213
TDE (Trickle-Down Effect)	160
TEU (Twenty Foot Equivalent Unit)	275
TFR (Total Fertility Rate)	160
THC (Terminal Handling Charge)	275
TiVA (Trade in Value Added)	161
TL (Total Loss)	275
TR (Trust Receipt)	275
TRS (Total Return Swap)	162
TS (Trans-shipment)	276
TSCS (Trans-Siberian Container Service)	276
TSR (Total Share Return)	162
TSR (Trans-Siberian Railway)	276
TT (Telegraphic Transfer)	276

TT (Transit Time)	277
TTC (Through Transport Club)	277
TUE (Trickle-Up Effect)	163
TVP (True Vapor Pressure)	277
TWRA (Transpacific Westbound Rate Agreement)	277
UB (Universal Banking)	163
UCP (Uniform Customs and Practice for Documentary Credits)	277
UE (Underground Economy)	164
ULC (Usance Letter of Credit)	278
USDI (US Dollar Index)	165
VAIC (Value Added Inducement Coefficients)	165
VAR (Value at Risk)	166
VC (Virtual Currency)	166
VE (Veblen's Effect)	167
VOC (Voice of Customer)	213
VOY (Voyage)	278
VSL (Vessel)	278
WA (With Average)	278
WACC (Weighted Average Cost of Capital)	167
WCS (Weight Surcharge)	279

WFG (Wharfage)	279
WLG (Wage-Led Growth)	168
WRS (War Risk Surcharge)	279
WT (Weight Ton)	279
YTM (Yield to Maturity)	168